A Century of *Ministry,* A Future of *Promise*

A 100TH ANNIVERSARY HISTORY OF THE

LITITZ CHURCH OF THE BRETHREN

1914 - 2014

by Donald R. Fitzkee

Arlin - Enjoy These pages from your past.

A CENTURY OF MINISTRY, A FUTURE OF PROMISE

A 100TH ANNIVERSARY HISTORY OF THE
LITITZ CHURCH OF THE BRETHREN
1914-2014
by Donald R. Fitzkee

Copyright © 2014

All rights reserved.

Cover photo: Rodney Moseman

Library of Congress Control Number: 2014915006
International Standard Book Number: 978-1-60126-432-9

Printed 2014 by
Masthof Press
219 Mill Road
Morgantown, PA 19543-9516

Contents

Foreword ix
Preface xi
Introduction xv

CHAPTER 1 | Beginnings 1

CHAPTER 2 | Church Life in Willow Street
        Meetinghouse 12
  Worship 12
  Love Feast 15
  Free Ministry 16
  Wise Admonitions and Public Confessions 21
  Avoiding Unbecoming Apparel 23
  Annual Deacon Visit 28
  Prohibition and Peace 30
  Early Events and Innovations 32
  Final Years at Willow Street 36

CHAPTER 3 | The Center Street Church:
        A Period of Rapid Change 38
  From Free Ministry to Paid Pastor 38
  The 1930s: Getting Organized 42
  James Moore: Winds of Change From the
        Windy City 45
  Disappearing Discipline 47

The Early 1940s: Focus on Europe 51
Youthful Energy: The Pastorate of Jacob Dick 57
Earl Bowman: Better Slow Than Rash 61
Floyd McDowell: "Behold, I Make All Things New" ... 64
Opening Wide the "Lamb's Book of Life" 66
We Would Be Building 70

CHAPTER 4 | The Orange Street Era:
    New Building, New Ministries 75
New Church, New Steeple, But Where Are
    the People? 80
Olden Mitchell: Ministering the Bread and Cup 81
Clem Rosenberger: A Turn Toward the Community ... 84
International Contacts 89
Beginnings of Successful Team Ministry 91
Charismatic Controversy 94

CHAPTER 5 | Jimmy and Ralph:
    The 1980s and 1990s 95
A Pastor First 96
Another Successful Team 97
More Deacons and Greater Commitment 101
Women in Ministry 105
Programs and Planning 107
People Spots 109
A Good Run 111
A Shelter in a Time of Storm 113
Refugees from Russia 119
Fighting Hunger 120
Other Outreach and Service 122
Closer to Home 123

>   Well Endowed 126
>   Music Notes 128
>   Adding a Second Service 132
>   A Deteriorating Building..................................... 133
>   Changing of the Guard 135

CHAPTER 6 | Ministry in the New Millennium 139
>   Assembling a New Team...................................... 139
>   Wednesday Nights ALIVE 142
>   A New Year's Tradition 143
>   A Nuevo Relationship 146
>   Focus on Families 148
>   Reaching Out and Bringing In 151

CHAPTER 7 | Daunting Challenges............................ 155
>   Beginnings of a Building Project 156
>   Time Crunch 160
>   Broken Ground and Busted Budgets 163
>   Retiring Debt: "Our Church Came Through" 169
>   How Will We Worship?....................................... 173
>   When Will We Worship?..................................... 177
>   Renewed Refugee Resettlement 182
>   Going Into the World.. 187
>   Excellence in Music 193
>   Youth Renovation... 194
>   Protecting Children... 197
>   New Vision, New Structure................................. 199

CHAPTER 8 | Where We've Been, Where We're Going .. 205
>   Reflections from 25 Years Ago 205
>   What About Today?.. 208

    Fewer People Doing More Work 211
    Increasing Age and Decreasing Attendance 211
    A Future of Promise? 214

APPENDIX A | Ministers and Moderators 217

APPENDIX B | Key Events 221

APPENDIX C | Membership and Average Attendance 224

APPENDIX D | 100th Anniversary Celebration Events 225

SOURCES CONSULTED 228

Sidebars

Between the House and Barn of John
    Dittman's Place 6
Learning to Read Music 13
Henry Royer Gibbel (1865-1927) 18
J. W. G. Hershey (1867-1929) 19
Barred by a Beard 23
A Poet, Too 36
Hersheys and Gibbels 39
Pioneers in Men's Work 52
Scouting in a Peace Church 83
I Won't Slow Down 85
A Lasting Imprint 87
A Precipitating Event 92
A Duck Tale 100
An Ongoing Commitment to Peace 114
Recycling When Recycling Wasn't Cool .. 118
The Making of a Hymnal 130
An Unwelcome Visitor 143
More Than a Statistician 153
A Stitch in Time Raised $60,000 170

Foreword

This history of the Lititz Church of the Brethren commemorates the 100th anniversary of the congregation. As a theme for the year-long celebration, the Anniversary Planning Team chose *Following in the Footsteps of Jesus: A Century of Ministry, A Future of Promise*.

As you read through these pages you will discover that the Lititz congregation has changed greatly since its early days, but one thing has remained constant—a desire to be faithful to Christ and follow in the footsteps of Jesus. As a church we can affirm along with David in Psalm 16:6, ". . . I have a goodly heritage." Through these hundred years God has blessed the Lititz church with many faithful servants who have helped guide and shape this congregation to meet the ever changing needs of our members and the world we are called to serve.

The readers of this book will find much to celebrate in the life of the Lititz church over the past 100 years. As we face the next century of ministry, however, the church will face new challenges. As our society moves toward a more secular and pluralistic future it will grow increasingly difficult to maintain our commitment to Christ and the church. But we have reason for hope.

Our future of promise is built upon the solid foundation of our past. No one can claim that this church was built upon anyone's individual efforts. Many members and church leaders contributed to the building of the church. In speaking of the church at Corinth, Paul said in I Corinthians 3, "I planted, Apollos watered, but God gave the growth. So neither the one who plants nor the one who waters is anything, but only God who gives the growth. . . . Each builder must choose with care how to build on it. For no one can lay any foundation other than the one that has been laid; that foundation is Jesus Christ."

While we celebrate our past and praise God for those who have gone on before us, it is Christ who is the true foundation and head of the church. All praise and honor and glory belong to Christ for anything that has been accomplished or will yet be accomplished. We dedicate this book and our 100 years of history to the honor and glory of God and for our neighbor's good. May we affirm with the hymn writer, "O God, our help in ages past, our hope for years to come."

Robert D. Kettering, Pastor

Preface

I was a couple weeks old when the Lititz congregation turned 50 in January 1964. I was a 25-year-old, recently married young man with a full head of hair when the Lititz Brethren celebrated their 75th anniversary in 1989.

And now, it's hard to believe that another quarter century has passed, but it must be true. My wife, Carolyn, and I celebrated our 25th wedding anniversary last summer, and I turned 50 this past Christmas. A lot has happened in 25 years in my life. All of my grandparents passed away. Carolyn and I started a family and have had the joy of watching our two children grow up. We bought two houses and moved twice during that time. I wrote two books, served two decades in the free ministry, made a career change, and the list goes on. A lot happens in a quarter century.

Which is why I was asked to write a new history of the Lititz Church of the Brethren. I wrote *The Transformation of the Lititz Church of the Brethren, 1914-1989*, a 75th anniversary history, in 1989. It was an opportune time. I was immersed in Brethren history as I prepared to write an account of Church of the Brethren congregations in Eastern Pennsylvania, which was published by Good Books in 1995 as *Moving Toward the Mainstream: 20th Century Change Among the Brethren of Eastern Pennsylvania*. Some of the Lititz history I studied ended up in the larger work, including the story of Lititz member Mayno Hershey, which served as the opening of the first chapter. It also was an opportune time because we were able to interview about a dozen older members of the congregation, who still had memories of the congregation's early days—people like Mayno, Laura (Hershey) Barwick, Ada Bingeman, Landis Stehman, Beatrice Mohler, Janet (Garman) Smith, Levi and Mary Weaver, and others. We couldn't interview those people today, but their memories were preserved and incorporated into this work, along with the memories and insights of a new generation of leaders that we interviewed this time.

It isn't often that an author gets an opportunity to rewrite history, but such is the case with me. This book incorporates most of the 75th anniversary history, with some changes and additions, including some photos and shorter articles that weren't included last time. But most of the new material in this book is from the past 25 years, covering the pastorates of Jimmy Ross and Ralph Moyer, and Bob Kettering and Steve Hess, along with a number of other significant pastoral leaders. During these years, the church completed and paid for significant building upgrades, navigated its way through changes in worship, including the painstaking process of adding a contemporary worship service and adjusting the Sunday morning schedule to try to satisfy the desires of the congregation, and much more. A number of Lititz saints went home to the Lord during this time.

So now we are up-to-date on our account of the Lititz Church of the Brethren, but it is inevitable that one day another history will need to be written. The church's life and ministry continue. If the church decides to do a new book for its 125th anniversary, I may be able to help. Lord willing, I'll be retired then and may need something to occupy my time. I'm less certain about my availability for the 150th anniversary history. The only thing I know for sure about that one is, if I do it, I want to be paid in advance.

    Donald R. Fitzkee
    June 2014

Introduction

If J. W. G. Hershey, early leader of the Lititz Church of the Brethren, were by some miracle to stroll into a service at today's Lititz church, he might be surprised by what he would see and hear. Before even stepping inside, he likely would frown and shake his head disapprovingly at the worldly steeple that so prominently protrudes above the roofline. He might even check the address to be sure he didn't inadvertently happen upon the Lutheran church down the street.

Once inside he would balk at the chandelier in the large gathering area and the stained glass windows in the tastefully decorated sanctuary. If he hadn't already begun, he would start to pray for the souls of the Lititz members when he heard organist John Huber light into a rousing classical prelude. During the announcements he might take the opportunity to stand up and admonish the brothers and sisters on the subjects of pride and worldly dress, and he certainly would scold the sisters for "bobbing" (cutting) their hair and neglecting to wear the prayer covering.

Wandering wide-eyed over to the family life center, he would puzzle over the spectacle of basketball nets in a meetinghouse and likely would clasp his hands over his ears as the praise team led out in song, accompanied by drums and electric guitar. By the time continental breakfast was served, he would be disillusioned with what his little Dunker congregation had become.

During the past 100 years the Lititz congregation has been transformed from a group of 119 plain-dressed brothers and sisters, meeting in an austere meetinghouse on Willow Street, into a congregation of 700 members, worshipping in a large and modern church building with features Hershey never could have imagined. A congregation that once went to great lengths to remain separate from "the world" now invites the world to come square dance in the church family life center. A congregation that once considered Brethren to be the only true church and discouraged its members from worshipping with "other persuasions" has been a leader in ecumenical cooperation through the local ministerium and the Lancaster County Council of Churches. So radical a transformation has taken place in the life of the church.

CHAPTER 1

Beginnings

The Brethren originated in 1708, when eight brothers and sisters were baptized in the Eder River in Schwarzenau, Germany. In 1719 the first group of Brethren migrated to the New World, seeking religious freedom and economic opportunity. The first Brethren settled near Germantown, north of Philadelphia. By 1724 enough Brethren had settled in Lancaster County to form the Conestoga congregation. As the Conestoga congregation grew and spread, it became more difficult for the scattered Brethren to come together to worship. So in 1772 the Conestoga congregation divided into three—Swatara, Conestoga, and White Oak. The Swatara congregation included Brethren to the north in parts of what would become Lebanon, Berks and other counties. White Oak incorporated Brethren primarily in the western part of today's Lancaster County, beginning just west of Lititz. In 1864, the Conestoga congregation again divided into three congregations—West Conestoga (now Middle Creek), Conestoga, and Ephrata. Brethren in Lititz became members of West Conestoga.

Writing in *Historical and Pictorial Lititz,* a 1905 town history, Rev. E. S. Hagen observed, "The history of Lititz—religious, educational, musical, social and industrial, is inseparable from the history of the Moravian Church in Lititz." Moravian leader Count Nicholas von Zinzendorf named the settlement "Lititz" in June 1756, after a town by the same name in Bohemia, where Moravians had sought refuge three centuries earlier. Moravians maintained a monopoly on all property ownership in Lititz until 1885, when a lease system that had prevented others from owning land was abolished.

The end of the lease system opened the community to the Brethren and others. By 1887, enough Brethren lived in Lititz to warrant construction of a meetinghouse. So a small frame house, 40-by-50 feet, with adjacent horse sheds, was built toward the eastern edge of town on Willow Street. (Today the building is located at 21 Willow Street and houses Word of Life Mennonite

Brethren in Lititz met in this simple frame meetinghouse on Willow Street from 1887 until 1926.

Fellowship.) The West Conestoga congregation met alternatively at five meetinghouses, so Sunday morning services likely were held in Lititz once every five weeks (once every six weeks after the Akron house was built in 1898). Ada Bingeman, who was born in 1904, recalled driving to the various meetinghouses with her uncle J. W. G. Hershey. "Uncle John had a two-seated carriage," she said. "Every six weeks we drove to Lanes." (Lanes, sometimes spelled Lehns, was one of the West Conestoga meetinghouses. Today it is a private residence located southeast of the Lancaster Airport on Kissel Hill Road.)

In 1888, John B. Gibbel secured permission to hold prayer meetings on Sunday evenings at the Lititz meetinghouse and at about the same time, despite objections, a Sunday school was organized by deacon Jacob S. Minnich. The Brethren tended to be suspicious of innovations such as the Sunday school, believing that the "family altar" in the home was the proper place for Christian education. Apparently the objections won out because the Sunday school was short-lived.

The Lititz Brethren renewed calls for a Sunday school in 1898, but the matter was deferred until 1900, when it was voted down 90-49. It was voted down again, 63-58, in 1902, before passing by a vote of 64-60 at an April 1903 meeting. All teachers were required to be "in order"—that is, they would follow the Brethren teachings on plain dress and other matters; a minister was to serve as superintendent; and all officers were to be elected by Council. By 1905 about 100 people were enrolled in the Sunday school, which met Sunday afternoons.

That same year a brief description of the Lititz "German Baptist Brethren" (as the Brethren were known until the name Church of the Brethren was adopted in 1908) was published in *Historical and Pictorial Lititz*, which provided some additional details about the church's life:

GERMAN BAPTIST CHURCH
by H. R. Gibbel

> The members of this denomination built a church in the Borough in 1887. It is a part of the West Conestoga District, which comprises five churches with about five hundred members. The preachers who serve the different churches are Revs. John Myers (sic, Myer), Lititz; Cyrus Gibbel, Brunnerville; David Snader, Akron; and E.B. Brubaker, at Brubaker. Regular services are held bi-weekly and prayer meeting every Wednesday evening and every alternate Sabbath evening. The church building is a good sized, substantial frame structure, located on Willow Street and there is ample shedding to accomodate (sic) the teams of members who attend services from the surrounding country.
>
> A Sunday School is connected therewith which holds its sessions every Sabbath afternoon and has about one hundred pupils. Rev. E. B. Brubaker is superintendent.

Referring to the Brethren ministers as "Reverend" likely was due to some Moravian editing, since Brethren generally did not use reverential terms for their leaders at that time, preferring the more biblical "brother."

A brief history of the Lititz congregation included in a 1926 Building Dedication program—perhaps penned by Henry R. Gibbel or J. W. G. Hershey—observed that Sunday school and prayer meetings "developed a consciousness of local unity and strength and gave encouragement to the sentiment that the Lititz church ought be an independent organization."

During the early 1900s the Lititz Brethren repeatedly requested permission to hold more frequent evening services at their meetinghouse. Some requests were granted, some not. The West Conestoga congregation met to call a minister on January 1, 1906, and the minutes report, "The lot fell on J. W. G. Hershey." He was called through an open election with no nominations, as was the custom. Later that year he became Sunday school superintendent and was elected delegate to Annual Meeting. Other early Sunday school leaders included Gibbel, who later became a minister, and deacon Henry Nies.

Deacon Henry Nies was an early song leader in the congregation.

Perhaps heartened by having a newly elected minister in Lititz, in March 1906 the Lititz Brethren asked to form a separate congregation. Their petition was postponed, and a committee was appointed to confer with surrounding congregations on the propriety of forming a new congregation. Though it isn't clear why, it appears the committee never organized to do its job. In July 1907, the request to form a separate congregation was voted down 92-77.

The brief 1926 history further explained the rationale for pursuing independence:

BETWEEN THE HOUSE AND BARN OF JOHN DITTMAN'S PLACE

Brethren congregations in Eastern Pennsylvania up until the 1930s or 1940s maintained distinct geographical parish boundaries. Church of the Brethren members were expected to attend the congregation within whose boundaries they resided, so the only way to switch from one Brethren church to another was to move to a different residence. Prior to the formation of the Lititz congregation, Route 501—known then as the Lancaster to Lititz Turnpike—was the dividing line between West Conestoga and White Oak. Brethren who lived on the west side of 501 were White Oakers. Those on the east side were West Conestoga members. Both West Conestoga and White Oak acted to spell out in some detail their side of the boundaries for the new congregation, as described in the Lititz congregation's January 1, 1914, Council Minutes:

PASSED BY WEST CONESTOGA:

Beginning at the corner of Broad and Market Streets, Warwick, Pa., thence along the public road to Brubaker's Cross Roads, thence along the Newport Road to Hess' Cross Roads, then along the public road to Bushong's Mill, thence to Henry Landis's, thence to Aaron Buch's, thence along the public road to the road leading from Kissel Hill to Millport near Wayne Grube's residence, thence through the fields and in a direct line to The Lancaster and Lititz Turnpike at the cross roads at Menno Brubaker's, thence northward along said Turnpike to the place of Beginning.

PASSED BY WHITE OAK

Beginning at Wissler's corner on the Lititz and Lexington Turnpike West along the road to the north east corner of Albert Shenk's farm, thence south along the road to Albert Shenk's lane, thence across the fields to Nathan Buch's corner, on Lititz Borough limits on the road leading from Lititz to Longenecker's farm, thence run line through between house and barn of John Dittman's place across the field to the Lancaster and Lititz Turnpike at Macpehla (sic) Cemetery, thence northward along the pikes to the place of Beginning.

A 1926 Building Dedication program spelled the boundaries out with more road names and fewer references to farms and barns:

The following boundary lines were decided upon: The Manheim road and market street formed the northern boundary; the road from Hess' meeting house to Bushong's Mill the eastern; an irregular southwestern line to the intersection of Peter's road and the Lancaster and Lititz turnpike the southern; the western boundary formed by the turnpike to Macpelah cemetery, thence a line northwest to the southwest corner of Lititz borough, then north along the borough limits to Manheim road.

In essence the new congregation's territory was comprised of the borough of Lititz and some additional territory to the south and east of town. Because the White Oak congregation's Longenecker meetinghouse was located just outside of the borough on Temperance Hill Road, Lititz territory to the west stopped abruptly at the borough line. The writer of a 1915 Eastern District history summarized, "The new congregation has a territory of almost four square miles, with a population of about four thousand."

As the number of Brethren in Lititz grew, there arose a feeling that an independent congregation ought to be formed here. It was inconvenient for those who lived in town to drive several miles into the country to service. Furthermore, there were families that had no team and found it impossible to attend Brethren services except the week when preaching was conducted at the Lititz house.

The Lititz Brethren continued to ask for more evening meetings in Lititz, and their requests were frequently refused. In March 1911, the matter of forming a separate Lititz congregation was again taken up, and a committee of three West Conestoga members and two White Oak members was appointed and instructed to discuss boundaries and draw lines. (The new congregation would be formed of territory from these two congregations.) Though the committee apparently did not come to agreement on boundaries, permission to organize was granted March 24, 1913. A new boundaries committee was formed. At a September meeting that committee was disbanded and yet another appointed. Eventually, an agreement on boundaries was reached.

During the Christmas season of 1913, Elder J. G. Royer, president of Mt. Morris (Ill.) College, preached a three-week-long series of revival services in the Lititz house "as a spiritual preparation for the organization" and stayed on to help organize the new congregation. (Another source says the series of meetings lasted just two weeks. Either way, by today's standards it was a lot of spiritual preparation!) At a meeting held New Year's Day, 1914, 52 present unanimously voted to form a separate congregation.

The congregation of 119 members was officially organized January 10 and elected I. W. Taylor, elder-in-charge; J. W. G. Hershey, clerk; and Nathan Brubaker, treasurer. Joining Hershey on the ministry team was elderly minister John W. Myer, who had been called to the ministry by the West Conestoga congregation in 1879, served as elder-in-charge of West Conestoga from 1900 to 1912, while also serving a stint as part-time pastor at Lancaster Church of the Brethren from 1902 to 1908. It isn't clear how active John Myer was in the new congregation. He is little mentioned in Lititz historical resources and the congregation chose Taylor as their non-resident elder-in-charge. Taylor was a member of a neighboring congregation and administrator of the Neffsville Home (later Brethren Village). He was well-known and highly respected in the district and denomination.

Deacons of the new congregation were George Shreiner, Nathan Brubaker, and Horace Buffenmyer. Henry R. Gibbel was named Sunday school Superintendent, overseeing an enrollment of 85.

Of the 119 charter members, 23 were former members of the White Oak congregation and 96 were from West Conestoga. The new congregation agreed to meet "each Lord's day morning" for Sunday school from 9:00 to 10:00, and "preaching" from 10:00 to 11:00.

The Lititz Brethren held their first love feast on June 6, 1914, in White Oak's Longenecker Meetinghouse. In September they met to call a minister. The election resulted in a tie, so both Harvey Eberly and Henry R. Gibbel were called. At the same meeting Henry Nies and John R. Gibbel were elected deacons. The minutes report that "all four, along with their wives, were installed that same evening."

In December the congregation held its first revival services. Eighteen people responded to the preaching of visiting elder I. J. Rosenberger and thus became candidates for baptism. After all the candidates were "privately interviewed and interrogated as to their faith," they were declared eligible for church membership and were baptized December 13 by I. W. Taylor in the small stream on the Linn Longenecker farm, the early baptismal site for the Lititz Brethren, which today is located at 820 Woodcrest Avenue, near Rohrer's Quarry.

> It was moved and carried that the new organization shall be known as the "Lititz Church of the Brethren."
> The following is a list of the members living within the lines of the new Organization.
>
> Brubaker, Lizzie M.
> Brubaker, Edna
> Breitegan, James
> Breitegan, Emma
> Bear, Lizzie
> Bollinger, Minnie
> Brubaker, Nathan
> Brubaker, Sarah B.
> Lizzie Becker
> Becker, Edna
> Becker, Anna
> Becker, Lizzie B.
> Bollinger, Catharine
> Brubaker, John
> Brubaker, Emma
> Badorf, Martha
> Bitzer, Annie
> Dittman, John
> Dittman, Estella
> Eberly, David
> Eberly, Sallie
> Eberly, Harry M.
> Eberly, Lizzie
> Erb, Ida
> Forney, Martin
> Forney, Annie
> Grant, Lizzie
> Gibbel, Henry R.
> Gibbel, Florence
> Gibbel, John R.
> Gibbel, Katie
> Gibbel, Paul
> Gibbel, Ella
> Groff, Ada
> Groff, Eva
> Groff, Violetta
> Froelich, Mary
> Hershey, Laura
> Hertzler, Jac. B.
> Hershey, J. W. G.
> Hershey, Lizzie R.
> Hershey, Laura G.

The list of 119 charter members, scanned from the congregation's original minutes, is shown here and on the facing page.

7

- Hossler, John
- Hossler, Emeline
- Keller, Allen
- Keller, Maria
- Keller, Lillie
- Lehn, Harriet
- Longenecker, Levi F.
- Longenecker, Minnie
- Longenecker, Christian
- Longenecker, Amanda
- Leed, John
- Long, Henry E.
- Long, Olivia
- Long, Nora
- Long, Henry
- Lutz, Edwin
- Lutz, Julia
- Miller, Emma
- Miller, John M.
- Miller, Amelia
- Myer, John
- Myer, Eliza
- Miller, Elizabeth
- Michael, Henry
- Minnich, Annie
- Myer, Clayton E.
- Myer, Anna
- Martin, William
- Martin, Maggie
- Meiskey, Mary
- Meiskey, Agnes
- Nies, Henry
- Nies, Ella
- Nies, Lottie
- Nies, Lucinda
- Rhode, Sarah
- Walter, Fanny
- Wissler, Lizzie
- Graybill, Barbara

- Nolt, Lizzie
- Reidenbach, William
- Reidenbach, Lizzie
- Reidenbach, Harry
- Royer, Harvey H.
- Royer, Ada
- Reinhold, Catharine
- Royer, Harry
- Royer, Ellen
- Schreiner, Geo. D.
- Schreiner, Fanny L.
- Sweigart, Maria
- Stehman, Isaac
- Stehman, Fanny
- Stehman, Clayton
- Stehman, Annie
- Stehman, Ellen
- Shenk, Lizzie
- Saylor, Susan
- Snavely, Mary
- Walter, Lizzie
- Wissler, Elba
- Wissler, Jacob
- Wissler, Agnes
- Witmyer, Lydia
- Withers, Elba
- Wahl, Hettie
- Weaver, Edna
- Wissler, Leah
- Young, Anna
- Young, Wayne
- Young, Susan
- Young, Katie
- Young, Callie
- Young, Ella
- Sturgis, Alice
- Weidman, Fanny
- Smith, Amanda

Seventy of the members were present, and forty-nine absent; there being a membership of 119.

CHAPTER 2

Church Life in Willow Street Meetinghouse

WORSHIP

The Willow Street Meetinghouse was a simple, rectangular structure, reflecting the value Brethren placed on simplicity in all things. There was no basement, no foyer, no steeple. Worship was equally simple, consisting of Scripture reading, prayer, singing, and preaching. The congregation always knelt for prayer (facing away from the front of the church, with arms propped on benches) and closed each prayer with the Lord's prayer. This was the practice as late as 1921 when a request came to Council Meeting to limit use of the Lord's prayer to once per service. The motion passed but was rescinded a short time later. Kneeling lasted longer; informed members agree that the congregation would regularly kneel for prayer until around 1950.

The hymns in the early services were lined (the leader would read one line, and the congregation would sing), often by Deacon Henry Nies, and sung *a cappella*, since the Breth-

LEARNING TO READ MUSIC

A 1965 district history book credits Harvey Eberly with teaching the Lititz Brethren to read music. Born in 1868 in a historic farmhouse north of Clay, Harvey developed an early interest in music. At age 18, he was the first of his extended Mennonite family to learn to read notes. At age 20, he began sharing his knowledge by leading a "singing school" on the third floor of a country store in the village of Durlach. Among the 50 pupils was a young lady from Lincoln named Elizabeth Minnich.

A few years later Harvey joined the Lititz Brethren. The history reports, "When he was 28 the Lititz Church of the Brethren decided to buy some song books with notes, and it was then that most of the members of this church learned to read music as a result of his teaching." If the source can be trusted, that means the Lititz Brethren would have been learning to read music in the late 1890s, when they still were part of the West Conestoga congregation.

There was one Lititz member that Harvey was unable to teach to read notes, Elizabeth Minnich. But it wasn't a total loss. The history reports, "Although she never became adept at reading music, she did marry her teacher four years later." And since Minnich is a "Brethren name," she likely had a role in bringing Harvey into the Lititz Church, where he later was called to the ministry.

Harvey M. Eberly

He also led singing schools—in both German and English—for nearly 50 years, and was listed in the district history as a congregational song leader and chorus and choir leader. While the math doesn't quite add up, the writer states, "Until he was forced to give it up at the age of 60, he was never without at least one singing class during all those years, never asking for a penny for his efforts."

ren opposed the use of musical instruments. Lining was necessary because the hymnal lacked musical notation, and most of the congregation likely did not know how to read music, anyway. Preaching was the focal point of each service. Ministers and deacons sat up front, facing toward the congregation. One minister was chosen to preach. "When the preacher stopped," recalls 84-year-old Ada Bingeman, "then a lot of the deacons had comments to make. It got a little tiresome!"

In the early years hymns were sung in German and English. Landis Stehman recalled in 1989, when he was 87, that periodically the entire service was conducted in German. "Every six weeks or so we'd have everything in German," he said. "I told my Dad, 'I don't feel like going.' I couldn't understand German. 'Well,' he said, 'go anyhow.'" So Landis went. Eventually the German services were discontinued, which suited Landis fine. As late as 1936 a request for "more German singing" came to Council.

Laura (Hershey) Barwick, the only surviving charter member of the congregation in 1989 and a daughter of J. W. G. and Lizzie Hershey, remembered how men and women sat on opposite sides of the church during services at Willow Street. But gradually the separate seating tradition was tested. "A young man would come to the ladies' side and sit with his girlfriend," she explained. "That's the way it started. Everybody stared at them and made them feel uncomfortable, but I don't think anything was done about it. And after somebody broke the ice, then it escalated." Even so, men and women sat separately, for the most part, as long as the congregation met on Willow Street, she says.

Another of J. W. G.'s children was among those who ignored the church seating chart. Hershey's son Abram married Catharine, a member of the Reformed Church in Brownstown. "She didn't like the fact that she and Papa could not sit together at first," says granddaughter Becky Hershey Becker. In order to avoid the withering glares and still sit together, they arrived late at church and sat in the back row. Habits die hard. A half century and two church buildings later Abe & Kitty continued to sit in the back row of the church on Orange Street. "This was a habit they continued to my grandfather's dying day in 1986," says Becky.

Love Feast

The love feast was the highlight of the year for the congregation at Willow Street. Eighty-two-year-old Beatrice Mohler remembered when love feast was an all-day affair. It began with the regular Sunday morning service and continued with the "self-examination service" in the afternoon. Based on 1 Corinthians 11, the minister encouraged members to examine themselves to be sure that they were at peace with God and their brothers and sisters in Christ before coming to the love feast tables. Most people stayed for a time of fellowship between the self-examination service and the evening love feast.

The order of the love feast service was similar to today's. The benches in the Willow Street meetinghouse were constructed so that every third bench could be converted into a table. The bench backs were reversible so that people sat on both sides of the "table." The meal consisted of bread and beef-rice soup. At Willow Street participants did not have individual soup bowls; four people ate from the same bowl. When the congregation moved in 1926 to a new building on Center Street, two ate from the same bowl. "The one who ate the fastest got the most to eat," said Janet (Garman) Smith, with a mischievous grin.

After the meal, the kiss of charity was passed around through the entire body of communicants. As early as 1922 a request came to Council to leave out this part of the service, perhaps because it was considered redundant. (The kiss also was passed during the feetwashing.) But the separate passing of the holy kiss persisted until 1934.

After the passing of the kiss came communion. Laura Barwick recalls that the ministers' and deacons' wives made the unleavened communion bread at the J. W. G. and Lizzie Hershey residence. The cup was a common cup or, more accurately, two common cups—one for the men and one for the women. Not until 1926 did a request for individual communion cups come to Council. It was promptly denied. After several other requests, in 1938 the congregation finally voted to use individual cups. Landis Stehman, who served many years as a deacon, said that sanitary concerns influenced the decision to use individual cups.

The afternoon self-examination service was discontinued in 1949. According to Landis, attendance for the service had gradually decreased and the logistics made things difficult for the deacons. The self-examination service lasted until after 4 p.m., and deacons needed to convert pews to tables and make final preparations for the love feast by 6 p.m.

Free Ministry

In January 1919, J. W. G. Hershey was elected elder-in-charge and Henry R. Gibbel church clerk. They, along with Harvey Eberly, John Myer, and, later, John W. Hevener (who in 1926 moved with his family into the Lititz congregation from Pocahontas County, West Virginia), served the congregation as free ministers. "Free ministry" was still common among the Brethren of Eastern District in the early 1900s and persists in a few Brethren congregations today. (The Eastern District of Pennsylvania was a forerunner of Atlantic Northeast District. In 1911 Eastern District was divided into Eastern and North Atlantic Districts. At a Special District Conference, held at the Lititz church in 1970, the two districts were reunited, forming Atlantic Northeast District.) Ministers were called from within the congregation and shared pastoral responsibilities. One minister was designated "elder-in-charge" and served as a head minister and moderator. Ministers earned their living through other employment and received no pay—except for occasional gifts—for their ministerial duties.

Both J. W. G. Hershey and Henry R. Gibbel were well-known in the community, the district, and beyond. Their families played active roles in the church. Both were schoolteachers in the Lititz area before forming the partnership of Hershey and Gibbel in 1890 and managing what was then called the Lititz Agricultural Mutual Fire Insurance Company. Both championed higher education in an era when many Brethren in Eastern Pennsylvania were suspicious of, or opposed to, it.

J. W. G. and Lizzie Hershey had 13 children of their own and raised two others. All those who survived attended college and went on to become teachers. Eventually many went into other professions. Laura Barwick, one of the Hershey children, observed, "Our family was unique in that there were so many children that all went to college." But, she pointed out, many other young people from Lititz were attending colleges in those early years of the church, which certainly must have set Lititz apart from neighboring Brethren congregations. (The 1965 Eastern District history included brief biographies of both Hershey and Gibbel, which appropriately enough appeared side by side on consecutive pages. They are reprinted below.)

HENRY ROYER GIBBEL
(1865-1927)

Henry R. Gibbel was born in 1865, the son of Elder John B. and Elizabeth Royer Gibbel. He attended Juniata College, then known as The Brethren's Normal School. He was baptized into the Church of the Brethren in Huntingdon, in 1885, and graduated from the Normal School in 1888. He taught the grammar school in Lititz for many years. He had a keen appreciation of literature, which overflowed into the lives of his pupils and gave them a true value of the printed page.

Mr. Gibbel was married to Florence Baker, of Lititz, in 1903, and they had one son, the late Henry Baker Gibbel.

He and J. W. G. Hershey were partners in business for 40 years, in the interests of The Lititz Mutual Fire Insurance Company. He was active in the organization of the Church of the Brethren in Lititz, and served as superintendent of the Sunday school for 25 years. In 1914 he was called to the ministry.

He had an unassuming friendliness with people. He liked folks and folks liked him. Because of personal relations and sympathetic understanding, he was a valuable counsellor and many people from near and far found their way to his home for guidance.

Henry R. Gibbel

At the time of his death in 1927 he was president of the Board of Trustees of Juniata College, a trustee of the Children's Aid Society, and of Bethany Biblical Seminary. He was elected president of the National Association of Mutual Fire Insurance Companies, held in Washington, D.C., two weeks prior to his death. He is survived by his wife and five grandchildren.

Supreme in his life was his Christian faith, which he professed openly and lived consistently. Henry Royer Gibbel served his generation well. (*History of the Church of the Brethren, Eastern Pennsylvania, 1915-1965*, p. 280)

J. W. G. HERSHEY (1867-1929)

J. W. G. Hershey was born in Penn Township, Lancaster County, on February 6, 1867, and grew up on a farm. He attended the local public schools and then took some courses at Millersville State Normal School in preparation for teaching.

He taught school in the Lititz vicinity and in the borough schools for a decade. In the classroom he is remembered for his thoroughness and for his strict discipline.

He married Lizzie R. Groff of the Bareville area and they had 13 children. They also reared two other children. In the home he was tender and considerate, but at the same time demanded immediate and absolute obedience. Despite an extremely busy life he found time to maintain daily family worship and to read to the family group the choicest poetry and extracts of local history. Some of the boys still know large portions of poems, like "Thanatopsis" and "The Raven," which they were required to commit to memory because their conduct failed to measure up to requirements.

In 1890 he and a fellow teacher in the Lititz schools and a fellow church member, Henry R. Gibbel, formed the insurance partnership of Hershey and Gibbel and took over the operation of the newly founded company, then known as the Lititz Agricultural Mutual Fire Insurance Company. With horse and wagon, they ranged over the county writing fire insurance and adjusting losses. They earned the reputation for prompt and generous settlement of claims. They lived to see the company grow and become the strongest mutual fire insurance company between Philadelphia and Pittsburgh.

He and his wife early affiliated with the Church of the Brethren. Because of his education and talents he was elected to the ministry and for a generation he helped bear the preaching burden at Lititz. He played an active role in the founding of the Lititz congregation and was its first church clerk. For over a decade, to the time of his death, he served the congregation as its elder-in-charge. Under his guidance the congregation grew and expanded. Despite the heavy demands upon his time from business, family, and local church, he still found time to conduct frequent revivals in the Eastern District of Pennsylvania. His home usually housed visiting ministers. After a busy day at the office and after the children were settled with their lessons, he and his wife would go visiting the sick and the aged in the local congregation. He also found time to serve on the trustee board at Elizabethtown College, on the local bank board, and to participate in many local business and cultural institutions.

J. W. G. Hershey

If he could be said to have had a hobby, it was fast and fractious horses. He loved nothing better than to drive a pair of horses that others found uncontrollable. Many a local person remembers the sight of J.W.G. in a rockaway carriage, with red beard flowing, driving at a high rate of speed. His control of horses was all the more remarkable because much of his adult life he labored under the handicap of one artificial leg.

He loved to ride over the county. There was scarcely a farm where he had not drawn the deed or mortgage, held a farm sale, or conducted a funeral service and he knew something interesting to tell of each place.

This background of intimate local contacts colored his preaching and though not a polished speaker he always was interesting and dynamic.

He died, May 31, 1929, at the age of 62, and is buried in Macpelah Cemetery in Lititz. His widow survived to her ninety-eighth year. (*History of the Church of the Brethren, Eastern Pennsylvania, 1915-1965*, pp. 281-282)

Wise Admonitions and Public Confessions

J. W. G. Hershey was known as a kind man, but a strict disciplinarian. If someone in the congregation whispered or talked while he was preaching, his daughter Laura recalled, "He would stop. He wouldn't go ahead. If they didn't stop talking, he would speak out. But he usually tried to [quiet them] with his piercing eyes."

As elder-in-charge from 1919 until his death on May 31, 1929, Hershey presided over Council Meetings. Some of the early Council minutes read like records of court proceedings. The Brethren had strict membership requirements and held members accountable to those requirements. Less than a year after the congregation began in 1914, its first member was disowned. The November 22, 1914, Council minutes report, "After the regular Sunday morning services [a sister] was disowned at her own request for fornication." In this particular case, the woman was reinstated two months later, after she married the father of her child, confessed, and requested pardon. Such incidents didn't always have such happy endings. Some people left the church rather than make a public confession.

Older members of the congregation can remember going to Council Meetings where people came before the congregation and confessed their sins. "It was a dramatic thing," said Laura, "to get up there in front of the whole church and make a public confession." Other behaviors for which members were disowned in the early years included drunkenness, disorderly conduct, and marrying while a previous spouse was still living. Longtime deacon Levi Weaver remembered that not all members kept Council happenings confidential. "When we had people confessing at open Council Meeting," he said, "it was all over town the next morning."

"They gradually realized that public confessions were not the kind of thing to do," said Beatrice Mohler. According to the minutes, people were disowned into the mid-1930s. In 1937 the congregation authorized the Official Board "to adjust such matters of irregular conduct on the part of members as the Board in its judgment feels should not be brought before the Council." It appears that in some cases the Board had already been using its discretion, but that decision likely ended the dramatic public confessions. The Official Board, however, continued to deal with matters of discipline into the late 1940s.

A 1940 case illustrates the practice at that time. In what was likely another fornication case, the minutes report, "The board forgave her on her confession to the pastor and his wife, the church having given them the right to do so in such cases." It is interesting to note that the special self-examination service prior to love feast was discontinued about the same time confessions to the Official Board ceased. By the late 1940s the church evidently had lost interest in regulating members' "personal lives."

But in the early years members had to be careful to avoid any number of taboo behaviors. Council Meetings frequently ended with "wise admonitions" from the elder-in-charge. The minutes of the March 15, 1916, Council report, "Elder Taylor gave a kind and fatherly admonition to the church against pride and worldliness." The March 16, 1921, minutes read, "After an admonition by the elder against stylish dressing and foolish wearing of the hair, the meeting was adjourned." In 1923 the congregation approved a recommendation from the Official Board "that our members be requested to keep away from carnivals and Sunday Base Ball."

Avoiding Unbecoming Apparel

In an effort to remain separate from the world and maintain modesty, the Brethren believed in a strict dress code, which included long hair worn under bonnets, no jewelry, and no makeup for the women, and plain cut coats and no neckties for the men. Levi Weaver shared that, when he was young, a deacon explained to him, "'When your heart gets right, these worldly things will fall off. You don't need

BARRED BY A BEARD

Even stricter requirements for appearance pertained to ministers. One thing that Henry R. Gibbel did not accomplish among his many other achievements was ordination to the eldership. In Gibbel's day, the ministry consisted of three levels. Ministers were called to the first degree—akin to licensed ministry—then advanced to the second degree and, after a number of years of faithful service, ordained an elder. Beginning in the early 1920s, J. W. G. Hershey, himself an elder, had advocated to the district elders for Gibbel's ordination. But there was one problem: Gibbel was either unable or unwilling to grow a proper Dunker beard. Eastern District leaders, backed by Annual Conference statements, refused to ordain an elder without whiskers. After years of stalling, the elders finally agreed in April 1926 "to make an effort" to ordain both Gibbel and fellow minister Harvey Eberly, who had no trouble meeting the beard requirement. The date was set for October 12, 1927, which turned out to be a little too late for Henry Gibbel. He passed away earlier in the week and was buried on the day he was supposed to have been ordained.

this long necktie and you don't need this lapel on your coat.'" The Brethren saw a clear connection between stylish dressing and the sin of pride.

It appears that most members of the congregation must have adhered to the dress requirements up until the mid-1920s, since the minutes scarcely mention dress-related issues before then. But members gradually began to violate the dress code. At the March 1926 Council Meeting concern was raised about some sisters not wearing the prayer covering at all times. One member said, "Steps should be taken to get members in order concerning the dress question, also that members stay away from worldly amusements." Another member raised concern about sisters wearing artificial flowers on their coats. A committee was appointed to deal with the concerns.

Members of the Sisters' Aid Society illustrate typical dress for women in the Lititz church during the 1920s. The sisters met on the second floor of the old "Hershey & Gibbel building" on Main Street, for lack of a suitable place in the meetinghouse. Pictured from left are: Lizzie Hershey, president; Mary Snavely; Amanda Bushong; Lizzie Brubaker; Kate Hoffer; Florence Gibbel, secretary; Fannie Weidman; Lizzie Wissler; and Mary Bruckhart.

CHURCH LIFE IN WILLOW STREET MEETINGHOUSE   25

This photo of a teen girls' Sunday school class at Lititz in the 1910s or early '20s shows the difference in dress between church members and those who had not yet joined. The church members wear plain dresses and prayer coverings with cap strings, while the others are dressed quite fashionably. Pictured are (front) Laura Hershey Barwick, Elsie Groff, (middle) Elizabeth Trimmer Raffensberger, Anna B. Wenger, Helen Niedermyer Heckman, (back) Thalia Hershey, and Anna Young Bomberger.

By March 1927 violations appear to have been widespread. One sister was admonished for wearing a gold ring. "Various complaints were brought before Council about wearing of unbecoming apparel and laying aside the prayer covering and continuing to trim their bobbed hair; even some have been seen attending at the theatre at Lancaster." The deacons were instructed to deal with these matters and to "kindly and lovingly admonish them to come within the bounds of the wise and reasonable rulings of the church." J. W. G. Hershey was apparently exasperated by the widespread flouting of the church's authority. The minutes report, "The Elder plead with the members sympathetically not to cause any offence to the Church and her Lord. On request he mentioned that waving of the hair was not becoming for any members and ought not to be done. He admonished strongly against attending and participating in questionable worldly amusements. We should have no desire to go, for it kills the desire for church services."

The admonitions apparently were ineffective because complaints about dress and participation in "sinful amusements" persisted. In fall 1928 Elder Hershey asked to be relieved because he no longer felt the support of the congregation. "He lovingly pled [sic] for sincere, spiritual cooperation." In January 1929 the congregation saw fit to re-elect him elder-in-charge, but he again asked to be relieved. The minutes report, "A number of members gave their expressions of feeling that Bro. Hershey should continue to serve, even tho [sic] things are not going as we would have them go." In a dramatic show of support, one member made a motion that all who were in favor of J. W. G. continuing as elder-in-charge should stand "and thereby pledge themselves to stand by him in his labors. Every member stood as far as the clerk could see."

J. W. G. died later that year, but complaints about women wearing hats and jewelry, "powder and paint," curling their hair, and not wearing the covering persisted. Other concerns were raised for more modesty, longer dresses, and the like. In 1933 one member called on sisters to wear their prayer coverings "when in society as well as in services," an indication that sisters were laying aside the covering during the week. One member asked the congregation to "take the Bible for our guide, not the world. Where will the Church be in ten years from now if we don't turn back and start over?"

As it turned out, 10 years later the church was at quite a different place. Concerns regarding dress (with the exception of an occasional plea for the prayer covering) had disappeared from the minutes by 1943.

Some of the congregation's older members in 1989 remembered back to those days of strict discipline and plain dress. Beatrice Mohler wore her covering and simple dresses all the time after she joined the church. She didn't mind wearing it to school and believed it had some value. "As far as I'm concerned," she said, "people did know you were supposed to be different."

Peggy Cassel looked at things differently. She put off joining the church because she didn't want to look "peculiar" at school. "I would have been interested in joining the church a couple years earlier than I did," she said, "because every night when I went to bed I was afraid I was going to die and go to hell. The reason I put it off so long was I was determined I wasn't going to wear a bonnet and I wasn't going to wear a covering to school." Finally her fears of eternal damnation got the best of her, and she joined the church in 1926 at age 13. She wore her covering to school the year of her baptism. "First thing I'd do every day when I got home from school was take that covering off!" she recalled. The next year she decided not to wear her covering to school. Once Peggy broke the ice, she said, many other Lititz Brethren girls stopped wearing their coverings to school.

Various members recall an episode where J. W. G. Hershey confronted a woman at the love feast table and told her she could not commune because she was known to wear a hat. Hats were considered worldly. "That caused a rumpus," Landis Stehman remembered. Most agree that J.W.G. didn't want to tell the woman she could not commune, but the Official Board members insisted that he do so.

Landis seemed to sum up the majority opinion of those members who remembered those days of strict discipline, when he said, "I wouldn't want to go back to it." Levi Weaver explained, "I think we still need to be disciplined, but it has to come from the inside. You can't discipline people from the outside and have a bunch of don'ts and rules. It has to come from within. It's pretty hard to discipline people when they are opposed to being disciplined and don't think they did wrong." The Lititz church learned that lesson during the 1920s and 1930s.

ANNUAL DEACON VISIT

Many of the complaints and concerns of members came to Council through the annual deacon visit. Each year deacons visited every member of the congregation and asked several questions to assess their standing with the church. At a Council in 1918 the Lititz Brethren approved seven questions to be included on a "visiting card" that would be used by deacons making their annual visit: "1. Are you still in the Faith of the Gospel as you declared when you were baptized? 2. Are you, as far as you know, in peace and union with the church? 3. Will you continue to labor with the Brethren for an increase of holiness, both in yourself and others? 4. When have you communed last? 5. How many church Councils did you attend during the last year? 6. Have you attended any prayer meetings during the past year? 7. Do you have a family Altar?"

Later the list likely was shortened to just the first three questions. The purpose of the visit was clearly to hold members accountable through this annual "spiritual check-up." The deacons usually were greeted at the door with the holy kiss. After some visiting, they asked the questions of each member and closed by kneeling in prayer. As part of the visit, concerns and queries were solicited for the March Council Meeting.

Beatrice Mohler observed that her family always looked forward to the deacon visit. "Of course, the house had to be cleaned," she said. She thought it was important for the deacons or someone from the church to get into the homes each year and establish a contact. She recalled that the deacon visit made her feel wanted and important. It let her know that the church cared about her spiritual well-being. Ada Bingeman agreed: "I know as a kid you were supposed to behave and be quiet," she said, when the visiting brethren came. "But we realized there was value to the visit."

Some members were less appreciative of the visit, however. The annual deacon visit persisted until 1939. In January 1940 someone questioned whether the visit should be continued. By a strong vote of 33-3 the congregation voted to continue the visit. But at the March Council, the deacons reported they were "unable" to make the visit. It isn't clear why. The Council instructed the deacons to "reconsider their report and fulfill their duty." But they elected not to continue with the visit, and the practice died.

Landis Stehman was a deacon prior to 1940, but he was unable to remember exactly why the deacons refused to continue visiting. He did recall that deacons were discouraged because people "weren't exactly telling the truth. Some of the folks would say, 'Yes, we're in the faith,' but the deacons knew that they weren't anyhow. It was a little shady there." Also, with the arrival of the congregation's first pastor in 1935, he assumed visiting responsibilities.

Prohibition and Peace

Prohibition was the social issue that commanded the attention of the Lititz Brethren in the early years. Twice, in 1914 and in 1915, the Lititz Council passed and mailed resolutions urging their legislators to vote in favor of specific prohibition bills. The 1914 resolution related to a national bill, and the 1915 resolution to a state bill. The Lititz congregation was passing political resolutions at a time when many Brethren still held convictions against political participation of any kind, even voting. Members such as Beatrice Mohler were involved in the Women's Christian Temperance Union as early as the 1920s.

In 1924 the Lititz Brethren addressed the peace issue in a letter to President Calvin Coolidge. The letter voiced the congregation's opposition to a proposal for a national "Mobilization Day," which apparently was to be a day of military parades and the like. The letter read as follows:

Dear President Coolidge:

As patriotic citizens of our beloved country and as devoted subjects of the United States for peace and good will, we the members of the Church of the Brethren do humbly desire to register our conviction against the proposed program of Mobilization Day September 12, 1924. We feel I) That the spirit of peace and good will should

CHURCH LIFE IN WILLOW STREET MEETINGHOUSE 31

In 1922 the congregation held its first Vacation Bible School. Minister Henry R. Gibbel & wife, Florence, are pictured back left.

be promoted in all our domestic and international relations and that such a military display might be easily misunderstood as a threat or provocation to other nations; II) That our display will have the psychological effect of instilling militarism into the youth of the land at the time when the rising tide of a spirit of good will and brotherhood of man is manifested. The members of our local organization numbering 247 communicants in the State of Pennsylvania in meeting assembled. . . this day of August 3rd, 1924.

Sincerely Yours,

J. W. G. Hershey, Presiding Elder
Henry R. Gibbel, Clerk

Early Events and Innovations

Several important innovations were made while the Lititz Brethren worshipped on Willow Street. In 1916 the congregation voted to establish a church library, with J. W. G. Hershey, Henry R. Gibbel, and Harvey M. Eberly serving as the "committee of censorship." In 1922 the congregation approved its first Vacation Bible School. Both of these innovations point to the premium the congregation placed on education.

In 1916 Emma Miller died, leaving $2,100 to the church. She was the first of a number of Lititz members to bequeath money to the Lititz church over the years.

In the early years the church's "music program" consisted entirely of *a cappella* congregational singing. But in 1925, Harvey Eberly organized a small male chorus. For a time, the congregation had a chorus, but didn't permit it to sing in church because of scruples against what they considered vain and performance-oriented "special music." "The chorus sang at other churches and for other occasions," wrote Paul Fahnestock in some historical notes about the chorus that he compiled from his father Nathan Fahnestock's records, "but not in our church."

The chorus grew—as did the congregation's musical outlook. After the congregation approved of "special singing" at the March 1926 Council Meeting, the Lititz men occasionally sang for their own congregation. Landis Stehman and others believed the mixed chorus also existed before 1926 and helped

Members of the Men's Chorus circa 1935: (front from left) Wilbur Garman, John Keller, Webster Bennis, Nathan Fahnestock, Harry Mohler, Harry Reidenbach, (second row) Nathan Heffley, Robert Keller, Burt Reidenbach, Martin Garman, William Garman, (third row) John Mohler, Ben Ritter, Elam Hollinger, director Ralph Gonder, Mahlon Garman, Landis Stehman, Galen Mohler, (back row) Stanley Becker, Samuel Becker, George Steffy, John Hershey, Landis Becker, William Bingeman.

create sentiment for special music during services. The mixed chorus was a forerunner of the adult choir.

The male chorus was reorganized in fall 1932 under the direction of Ralph W. Gonder with 18 singers. Serving as President was John G. Hershey. Nathan Fahnestock was secretary. During the final two months of 1932, the chorus sang six different times, including at area revival meetings, on a WGAL radio broadcast, and for Sunday worship at Lititz on Christmas Day. Three additional members were added to the chorus "by unanimous consent" in 1933. That year the male chorus sang no less than 18 times in various venues, including the Church of the Brethren Annual Conference in Hershey. Ralph Gonder declined to lead the chorus in September 1936, citing a need to spend evenings earning more money for his family. The chorus convinced him to return in January 1937 by offering him a salary of three dollars per month, likely making him the church's first paid music leader. By 1938 the chorus had swelled to nearly 40 voices. Paul Fahnestock remembered annual male chorus picnics as social highlights each year.

In June 1926 the congregation voted to form a Young People's Society, the first church youth group at Lititz. Other early groups in the church were the Christian Workers, who met weekly for Bible study and fellowship, and the Sisters' Aid Society. The congregation also held weekly prayer meetings in the early years, which were well-attended, said Beatrice Mohler. Those services were interrupted during 1918 because World War I had produced a coal shortage.

FINAL YEARS AT WILLOW STREET

During the 1910s and '20s the Lititz congregation grew steadily. By 1924 the membership had more than doubled to

247 members and the building at Willow Street was becoming inadequate. The meetinghouse was small and had no facilities for Sunday school. Most classes met in the sanctuary all at one time. Some found quieter locations. "Back at Willow Street, my Sunday school class was in a Packard automobile," said Landis Stehman.

In 1917 the Finance Committee had been instructed to establish a building fund. In 1922 a Locating Committee was authorized to purchase a site on Center Street and a committee was appointed to plan for a new church building. The congregation approved plans prepared by Reading architects Richter and Eiler in April 1923. The new building was to have room for 460 worshippers in the auditorium and Sunday school space for 501 pupils. But the building matter was not yet settled. Apparently, there were points of contention, reflected in the unsuccessful attempts to raise funds. In July 1924 the Council voted to rescind all previous minutes on the building issue, disband the present Building Committee to save it "from any further embarrassment," and appoint a new committee. It appears that not all members were satisfied with the Center Street location.

The new committee recommended building on the Center Street site anyway, and approved a modified version of the architect's plans. The Center Street church was dedicated during services held November 25-28, 1926. Notable preachers at the dedication services included Elder Rufus Bucher, Elder James M. Moore (who several years later would become the Lititz congregation's first full-time pastor), Frank Carper, Howard A. Merkey, Elder Henry K. Ober, and Elder Samuel G. Meyer. The cost of the building was $61,887.79. At the time of the dedication, church membership was 227.

A POET, TOO

Not only was J. W. G. Hershey a successful minister, businessman, and community leader, but he also dabbled in poetry. He penned this poem for the dedication of the new Lititz churchhouse on Center Street in 1926. The emphasis on peace is interesting in light of the fact that Hershey was growing exasperated with the lack of unity in the congregation as members' commitment to plain dress was waning.

At last, at last, in calm surprise
    Our prayers and hopes we realize
To enter in and to possess
With joy and peace we can't express,
    God's House of peace, peace, peace.

The former house has served its day,
    For the latter house we now all pray
That the peace and glory possessed by the old,
    The new may increase a hundred fold,
In peace, peace, peace.

Our hearts were often there made glad,
    When the world and lust had made them sad;
but when we met, as we often did
    In prayer and praise and fellowship,
We had peace, peace, peace.

This house, it stands on higher ground;
    In size and beauty doth abound,
but that alone will not suffice
    Unless we serve and sacrifice
For peace, peace, peace.

If we wish the approbation
> God's favor, also confirmation,
We must lay ourselves and all
> On the altar, great and small
For peace, peace, peace.

Our hearts must be yearning
> To see the bush burning,
And hear God's voice calling,
> Though the sound be appalling
To peace, peace, peace.

May our hearts in union blend,
> Our FAITH hold out until the end.
Our toils, our sufferings, and cares,
> Shall be no hindrance to our prayers
for peace, peace, peace.

> > > J.W.G.H.

CHAPTER 3

The Center Street Church:

A PERIOD OF RAPID CHANGE

The step from the Willow Street Meetinghouse to the Center Street church was a big one. Situated in a new, modern facility, the congregation was poised for change.

FROM FREE MINISTRY TO PAID PASTOR

The period immediately following the move to the Center Street church seems to have been turbulent and transitional. In 1927 Henry R. Gibbel died. During 1928 J. W. G. Hershey made it known he wanted to be relieved of his duties as presiding elder. In 1929 he died. Elder Nathan Martin, of Lebanon, was elected as the new presiding elder. Harvey Eberly was named foreman, or assistant elder.

Within a two-year period the congregation had lost its two primary leaders. Rather than calling new ministers from within the congregation, they looked to the outside for

HERSHEYS AND GIBBELS

Though early minister J. W. G. Hershey fathered 13 children, today few Hershey descendants remain in the congregation. According to J. W. G. Hershey's great-granddaughter, Becky Hershey Becker, of the 13 children born to J. W. G. & Lizzie Hershey, Christian, Naomi, and Susan died in infancy; Robert died of pneumonia eight days past his fourth birthday; Helen passed at age 11 from heart-related issues; and Henry also succumbed to pneumonia at age 32, just months before his father's death. All who survived attended college and all but one taught for a time in public schools. Of the seven surviving children—Mary, Owen, John, Laura (Barwick), Abram, Isaac New-

This photo of members of the J. W. G. and Lizzie Hershey family appeared in the January 10, 1973, Lititz Area Edition of the Shopping News *with a note that the photo had been taken 50 years ago. An accompanying article provided information about the family.*

ton, and Louetta (Weaver)—most followed careers and spouses to other places and other churches, scattering from Eastern Pennsylvania to California. Of those who remained in the area, only John and Mayno and Abram and Kitty settled into the Lititz church. Laura Barwick and husband, John, returned to the congregation late in life after many years serving overseas among refugees and the poor. (John Workman Barwick's distinguished career earned him an entry in *The Brethren Encyclopedia*.) Today, of the once considerable Hershey clan, only two great-granddaughters of J.W.G. and Lizzie Hershey (Becky Hershey Becker and Christine Bomberger) and three great-great-grandchildren remain members of the congregation.

In contrast to the Hersheys' large family, Henry R. and Florence Gibbel had but one child, Henry B. But today the congregation has a number of Gibbel descendants (all of the Gibbels with the distinctive G-I-B-B-E-L spelling). In fact, in its first century the congregation has never been without at least one Henry Gibbel. Currently it has three of them: Henry R.'s grandson Henry H. Gibbel, great-grandson Henry R. Gibbel, and great-great-grandson Henry A. Gibbel, who goes by Alex.

leadership. Beatrice Mohler suggested that no member of the congregation stood out as a candidate for ministry, and the remaining ministers lacked the necessary skills to take a central leadership role. "Maybe no one was qualified," she theorized. At least no one in the congregation could provide the high quality of leadership that the congregation had grown accustomed to with Hershey and Gibbel. Perhaps as a result of the leadership vacuum, membership declined in 1927 and didn't rebound decisively until 1932, when it jumped from 239 to 277.

The question of hiring a full-time pastor was raised for the first time in March 1930, but was deferred indefinitely. The following March several ministry-related concerns were brought to Council. There were requests for a part- or full-time pastor, more "spirit-filled sermons," and more visiting of the sick by ministers. One member stated bluntly, "We need the help of a pastor or a younger minister." The pastor question was raised again in March 1932, but no action was reported.

Finally, in July, following a lengthy discussion, the congregation voted to hire a part-time pastor. Three visiting elders, Samuel H. Hertzler, Nathan Martin, and John I. Byler, Sr., spoke in favor of hiring a pastor. Visiting elder I. W. Taylor expressed reservations, and Deacon Henry Nies opposed the move on financial grounds. At the same meeting, Byler was elected elder-in-charge. In August 1932 the congregation invited A. C. Baugher, academic dean at Elizabethtown College, to preach once a month at Lititz as part-time pastor. The following spring Baugher was elected elder-in-charge. Baugher served as part-time pastor until September 1, 1935, when the congregation's first full-time pastor arrived. (The 1965 *History of Eastern District* states

A. C. Baugher, the first part-time pastor at Lititz, later would become president of Elizabethtown College.

that Baugher, Byler, and Martin all were part-time pastors, but that doesn't seem to be the case. A. C. Baugher was the only one of the three to be called "pastor" in the congregation's Board and Council Meeting minutes. Both Martin and Byler served as elder-in-charge of the congregation, receiving modest pay for their services, which included occasional preaching. The fact that they were paid does not mean that they were part-time pastors. It was the Lititz congregation's practice to pay small amounts to outside elders-in-charge, beginning with I. W. Taylor, who received $20 in 1915.)

The part-time pastor arrangement sufficed for a few years, but in March 1935 requests for a full-time pastor came to Council, and a Search Committee was appointed. In May the congregation approved a $6,000 budget—its first—and recommended the appointment of "a committee of at least twenty to personally solicit each member (Deut. 16:17) of the Church and invite and urge them to use the envelope system as the best method (I Cor. 16:2) of systematic giving. . . . " James M. Moore, of Chicago, Ill., was called by a plurality vote as pastor at a starting salary of $1,800. Lititz thus became one of the earlier churches in the Eastern District to hire a full-time pastor. At a single Council, the congregation approved its first budget, its first every-member solicitation campaign, and its first full-time pastor.

The 1930s: Getting Organized

In the midst of the pastoral debate in the early 1930s Lititz Brethren took a number of other steps toward becoming a more typical Protestant church. Around 1928 the congregation began baptizing some new members in the baptismal pool at the Lancaster Church of the Brethren, rather than in icy streams.

Circa 1930 the congregation prepared an annual schedule of events, and in 1933 it was decided to make a list of inactive members and try to contact them. Some had moved away and their whereabouts were unknown. In 1934 the congregation published its first congregational directory and elected its first Board of Christian Education. Florence Gibbel, wife of Henry R. Gibbel, was elected "chairman," and Edna Mohler secretary.

The new Board had rather broad responsibilities, overseeing the entire Christian education program and other areas not directly linked to Christian education, such as appointing choristers for revival meetings and lining up special music. This Board apparently gave voice to the growing interest in missions at the Lititz church. One of the first events planned by the Board was an Institute of Missions, led by C. D. Bonsack, Missionary Secretary of the Church of the Brethren, and Nigeria missionary A. D. Helser.

Christian education was one area in which the women of the church took active leadership roles from the very beginning. (Women could not be deacons or ministers, which also excluded them from the Official Board.) Florence Gibbel was extremely active in the Christian education program of the congregation and district. Florence was Lutheran before she married Henry R. Gibbel and joined the Brethren. She was a Sunday school teacher, church correspondent to the *Gospel Messenger*, Bible school director, and held a host of other positions. Many older members in 1989 remembered having Florence as their

Sunday school teacher. "Florence Gibbel was my mentor," said Beatrice Mohler. "She was my good friend and she helped me a lot. We worked together in the Missionary Society and the Vacation Bible School, and a lot of things. It got to be that I called her 'Ma Gibbel.'" Beatrice later took on many of these responsibilities.

"Ma Gibbel" may have been the first woman Annual Conference delegate elected by the Lititz church, and she also was deeply involved in district functions, such as the Women's Fellowship. According to the 1965 *History of Eastern District*, she served as District Secretary of Women's Fellowship, "providing leadership, inspiration, and guidance during the formative years of 1923 to 1943. Upon her retirement from that position, she was named honorary president." She also was a leader in the district's youth work and camping movement, and served many years on the Board of Trustees of Juniata College.

Florence Baker Gibbel

Lititz felt strong ties to the Brotherhood, Bethany Biblical Seminary, the district, and Elizabethtown and Juniata Colleges during the early 1930s. Frequently groups such as "Student Volunteer Bands" (like deputation teams) came from the colleges, along with their *a cappella* choirs. Also, faculty members from Elizabethtown, Juniata, and Bethany Bible School came to speak. The Lititz church supported these institutions faithfully.

James Moore: Winds of Change From the Windy City

James M. and Ella Moore arrived September 1, 1935, from Chicago. The Lititz congregation's first full-time pastor, Moore was a graduate of Mt. Morris Academy and Bethany Biblical Seminary. He had served on the Bethany Board of Directors, taught Old and New Testament at the seminary, and was well-known in the entire Brotherhood. He was Annual Conference moderator in 1930 and had served on several Annual Conference committees.

The 10 years of James Moore's pastorate were good ones for the Lititz church, as membership grew from 301 in 1935 to 418 in 1945. A number of important changes took place, some of which probably can be attributed to the influence of

A signed Christmas card from Pastor James M. and Ella Moore.

a pastor who came from outside of conservative Eastern District.

Less than a month after Pastor Moore's arrival the congregation voted to cooperate with "other churches in the town of Lititz" for a Thanksgiving service—the first evidence of ecumenical involvement in the life of the Lititz congregation. The following March a request came to "have services on Thanksgiving day in our church as before," an apparent reaction against the ecumenical service. No action was taken. In 1936 the congregation participated in a pulpit exchange. Pastor Moore preached in the Lutheran church and J. C. Light, a United Brethren minister, preached at Lititz. Apparently not all members were convinced of the propriety of ecumenical involvements; in 1938 the Official Board considered joining in "Union Meetings" (interdenominational services) in Lititz but decided against it. The ecumenical involvement that began with James Moore, however, continued through the years.

In 1936 Pastor Moore began the congregation's first newsletter, the *Lititz Messenger*, which was published at least until 1948. Also in 1936, permission was granted to begin Women's Work at the local level; the congregation's first "General Sunday School Outing" was approved; and Pastor Moore was elected elder-in-charge, replacing A. C. Baugher. The congregation formed a local Pastoral Committee in 1937, as Annual Conference had recommended. Individual communion cups were first used in 1938.

A committee was appointed in January 1939 to study the "special music question." Special music, which had been approved in the late 1920s, apparently had become more prevalent. Several requests for more congregational singing had come to Council in the interim, evidence that some people thought special music was playing too prominent a role. At the March Council, the committee's report was adopted, thus forming a permanent five-member Music Committee to administer the special music program. The report also set forth goals and purposes of special music and called for the establishment of a church music fund.

At the same meeting, the church approved the use of the first musical instrument in the Lititz church—a harp at the wedding of Franklin Cassel and Margaret (Peggy) Miller. The congregation voted to grant the request for the harp "with the understanding that the granting of the request applies in this case only." Franklin recalled in 1989 that he wasn't sure permission would have been granted for a piano at that time but, he said with a grin, "They could hardly refuse a harp." In December 1940 the Council granted a request for an "organ or similar instrument" to be used at a wedding. Again it was emphasized that the ruling applied to this case only. Finally, in March 1943, Council gave blanket approval for musical instruments at weddings and other special occasions, under supervision of the Music Committee. Requests no longer had to come to Council.

The church installed its first baptismal pool in 1940. It appears that the way to get things done in the Lititz church was to offer to pay. Such was the case with the baptismal pool. It was approved with the understanding that "a certain member promises to pay the bill." The bill for the baptistery and an additional stairway came to $511.42 and was paid by Sister Susie Royer. Her husband, Clayton, had made the promise, but died two weeks before the April 24, 1940, dedication service.

Disappearing Discipline

Perhaps more significant than all other changes in the 1930s was the congregation's shifting attitude toward discipline. At a March 1935 meeting of the Official Board a deacon reported, "The Mennonites are complaining that our church's looseness as to discipline gives them a lot of trouble among their younger members."

Fewer concerns regarding dress and behavior of individuals were registered at each March Council as the years progressed. The ones that were expressed often were not addressed. The March 1936 Council, the first spring Council after Pastor Moore's arrival, seems to have been a turning point. The deacons brought 21 suggestions and two requests, received from members during the annual visit. A few of the more significant ones included suggestions that "no sister with bobbed hair should take a public part in public worship;" and "sisters should wear prayer coverings at all times, not only at Church." Another member cautioned the brothers and sisters "not to drift into popular fashions of the world," but to "keep ourselves unspotted from the world." Another stated bluntly, "I do not think our members and Sunday school teachers should go to the moving picture show." No action was taken on any of these matters, not even so much as an admonition from the elder.

The last public confession at a Council Meeting came in March 1937. The congregation voted to forgive a sister of adultery after she made a "noble confession." After 1937 the pastor and the Board heard other confessions, but it appears that the Board no longer recommended disowning. A case handled at the September 8, 1937, Council shows how much the congregation's attitude toward discipline had changed. At that meeting the church voted to retain as a member a man who divorced and remarried while his former wife was still living. James Moore served on the two-member committee that drafted the recommendation approved by Council:

We, the committee appointed by the Official Board on August 16 to investigate matters regarding Bro. _____, have carefully and prayerfully considered the whole matter, and recommend the following action: 1. We reaffirm our acceptance of the Scripture teaching on the sanctity of the marriage contract, that what 'God hath joined together, let no man put asunder.' 2. In light of the Scripture and Annual Conference decisions, we cannot sanction or approve of a marriage while a former companion is living. 3. In the case of Bro. _____, we have taken into consideration all the circumstances as we know them, including Bro. _____'s attitude and his expressed desire to remain with the church, as well as Conference decisions and the attitude of the Brotherhood in general and also of the Lititz congregation. We recommend as follows: (a) That the responsibility of this union be left between Bro. _____ and God. (b) That the church bear with the situation, and permit him to remain and work with the church in the laity. (c) That Bro. _____ be urged to a continual growth in consecration to God and the fullest possible harmony with the doctrines and practices of the church.

The errant brother was limited to being a part of the laity of the church, but he was retained as a member nonetheless.

The story of Mayno and John Hershey further illustrates how much the Lititz congregation's attitude toward discipline changed during the 1930s. John Hershey was the son of J. W. G. Hershey. John had left the congregation to attend Bethany Biblical Seminary and the University of Chicago. Mayno had grown up in a Church of the Brethren congregation in Ohio, where the Brethren placed less emphasis on dress and discipline.

When John and Mayno came to Lititz in 1929, the church would not accept Mayno as a member. "I was wrong on eight counts," she recalled in 1989. The Lititz Brethren objected to her bobbed hair, her gold ring, her card playing, the fact that she didn't wear a prayer covering all the time, she didn't dress plain, and she did wear a hat. She doesn't recall her other "offenses." John also created a stir. He was discussed at meetings of the Official Board. The May 26 minutes report, "Brother John G. Hershey was talked about quite freely as to his teaching and preaching and with regard to his modernistic spirit and way of living." Later that year, the Board decided that he should not be allowed to teach.

Mayno Hershey (left) and Laura Barwick, 1985. The congregation wasn't ready to accept Mayno's "worldly" ways when her husband, John, introduced her to the congregation in 1929. She later became an active leader in the congregation.

Mayno finally joined the church in 1937, eight years after her arrival. She had not modified her "objectionable" behaviors during that time; the congregation had relaxed its expectations. In 1941 she held an office in the Women's Work. John became church clerk in 1943. Both Mayno and John held many positions of responsibility in the church over the years and were among the advocates for change in the Lititz congregation. But the Lititz church wasn't ready for them in 1929!

When the annual deacon visit was discontinued in 1939, members were no longer asked if they had specific suggestions or requests to bring to Council. They were forced to take the initiative in bringing items to Council. As a result, suggestions regarding dress and personal behavior—so common to the church Councils during the congregation's first 25 years—virtually disappeared overnight.

To the east and west of Lititz, the more conservative Middle Creek and White Oak congregations—served by free ministers even today—maintained stricter standards. As geographical boundaries between congregations were less rigorously enforced during the 1940s and beyond, Lititz sometimes picked up members who were fleeing discipline of neighboring congregations. In a 1988 letter to the author, Ernest Shenk observed, "Lititz attracted many who did not desire to abide by the rules of neighboring congregations who practiced strict discipline."

The Early 1940s: Focus on Europe

During the early 1940s the Lititz congregation focused much attention on events in Europe. In 1938 the congregation took an offering for "neutral relief" to aid war sufferers in Spain and Japan. (The relief efforts in Spain spawned the idea of what today is Heifer International.) In 1941 the denomination's Brethren Service Commission met to discuss the funding of civilian camps for conscientious objectors. A Special District Meeting, moderated by James Moore, was held to discuss the matter, and the churches of Eastern District agreed to support the camps. Beginning in 1941, the Lititz deacons solicited funds from members to support these Civilian Public Service camps, and the congregation took a number of offerings for Brethren Service.

In 1942, in response to a request from the Red Cross, the church agreed to provide its basement for a detention place for refugees and others, if such action should become necessary. By February 1944 the Lititz congregation was active in the district's "Heifers for Relief" project. The Lititz Men's Work coordinated the project, while various individuals and groups in the congregation were sponsoring 10 heifers at the time.

The Lititz Brethren's involvement in World War II didn't end with their participation in relief efforts. Many of Lititz's young men entered the military. Others chose alternative ser-

> ### PIONEERS IN MEN'S WORK
>
> Up until the early to mid-1900s ordained elders, ministers, and deacons ruled the roost in Church of the Brethren congregations, districts, and the denomination as a whole. Beginning in the 1920s, laymen began to desire a more active role in the work of the church. The 1926 Annual Conference of the Church of the Brethren gave the nod to the organization of a denominational Men's Work organization. The following June, Men's Work got organized at its first national convention, held in Hershey, Pennsylvania. Ironically, though this first meeting was held within the bounds of the Eastern Pennsylvania District, it would

take the conservative leaders of the district another dozen years before they would officially approve, perhaps out of concern that the new organization would undermine their authority. The 1939 District Meeting finally approved the formation of a District Men's Work Council. But not everyone had waited for their okay.

Lititz layman James Breitigan had served on the national Men's Work Council almost from the beginning and kept the men of the Eastern District informed of all the work laymen were doing in the church. Lititz was one of two congregations to organize local Men's Work organizations before they were officially sanctioned by district leaders. When the new District Council was formed in 1940, Breitigan was one of the three elected to serve, and he would remain a driving force until his death.

Men's Work later was renamed Men's Fellowship. For many years local, district, and denominational Men's Work programs spearheaded local service projects, raised money for evangelism and service ministries, and gathered for fellowship activities. Projects during the 1940s included contributing money and labor to help establish Camp Swatara; and donating grain, seeds, powdered milk, and heifers for relief after World War II.

According to the 1965 *Eastern District History*, "In 1947 the pioneer of Men's Work in the District, James H. Breitigan, passed away. During his extended period of illness he held many bedside conferences and gave many helpful suggestions. He rejoiced greatly in the progress which had been made but saw the urgent need for increased lay leadership in the church." Thus two Lititz members, Breitigan and Florence Gibbel, were key figures in the formation of Men's and Women's Work, respectively, in Eastern Pennsylvania.

vice as conscientious objectors (COs). Pastor Moore regularly corresponded with some of the young men in the military, and all those who were away received the church newsletter. It doesn't appear that the congregation attached any stigma to military service, despite the Church of the Brethren's opposition to war. Harry Badorf, who volunteered for the Navy in 1948 to avoid serving in the Army, recalled in 1989, "It was strongly suggested that the CO approach be taken." But he doesn't recall anyone confronting him on his decision to enter the military. Generally, the church left the decision up to individuals and supported them whether they chose to fight or conscientiously object.

Over the years, well over 20 Lititz members chose to give a year or more of their lives in church-related service work.

While many Lititz members were away from home because of the war, the ones who stayed behind weren't sitting still. In August 1939 the congregation approved a request from the trustees to build a parsonage next to the church. The congregation built its first parsonage for about $6,500.

Musical instruments continued tiptoeing toward the sanctuary. In 1943 instruments had been approved at weddings, under supervision of the Music Committee. In January 1944 the young people were given a room in the basement and were given permission to place a piano there, "with no expense to the church." In September the young people were given permission to accept an organ as a gift. So by fall of 1944 instruments were used regularly at weddings in the sanctuary, and the church basement housed both a piano and organ, just one short step from permanent placement in the sanctuary.

In fall 1940 a number of suggestions were offered to improve the love feast. Among them was that communicants should receive individual soup bowls, and that steps should be

THE CENTER STREET CHURCH 55

The congregation worshipped in this building on Center Street (pictured inside and out) from 1926 to 1962, when the congregation relocated to the present Orange Street location. The brick parsonage next door was added in 1939.

taken to speed up the feetwashing. A committee was appointed to consider and implement the changes. In January 1943 more dissatisfaction with the love feast was voiced and calls were renewed to hasten feetwashing. Apparently by the time members returned from washing feet in the basement, the individual bowls of soup were cold. Eventually the feetwashing was held after the meal.

James Moore announced his resignation at the January 1945 Council, effective August 31, 1945. According to Mayno Hershey, Moore was the perfect first pastor. Back in 1935 not

The Lititz congregation held a mortgage burning service for the Center Street building on July 29, 1945. Pictured (from left) are Noah Trimmer, Amos Geib, Landis Stehman, Pastor James Moore, and Allen Keller.

all Lititz members had been convinced that it was right to pay a pastor to do the Lord's work. Some opposed the new pastor. But, according to Mayno, "the people who had been opposed to him didn't want to accept his resignation (10 years later). I thought that was the greatest tribute that could ever be paid to a pastor."

Youthful Energy: The Pastorate of Jacob Dick

Moore was 70 years old when he resigned. He cited his age and physical limitations, and his inability to deal effectively with the youth as reasons for resigning. He felt it was time to pastor a smaller church! In April 1945 the congregation called Jacob T. Dick as their new pastor. A graduate of Juniata College and Bethany Biblical Seminary, Dick left a pastorate at the Shade Creek congregation, in Western Pennsylvania, and began his Lititz pastorate October 15. He was 27 years old when he and his wife, Leona, arrived. Norman K. Musser was elected elder-in-charge on August 15, 1945.

In its early years the Lititz congregation believed that the Church of the Brethren was the one true Christian body. This attitude slowly evolved over the years and the congregation gradually came to accept the validity of other Christian denominations. Ecumenical cooperation had begun shortly after James Moore's arrival in 1935. Yet, when Pastor Dick arrived in 1945, the Lititz congregation still maintained barriers to ecumenical cooperation. Members of other Christian denominations could not commune with the Lititz Brethren, and the congregation would not transfer memberships to other denominations.

During the early 1940s it was common for the congregation to cancel membership of those who had joined with other denominations. In November 1945 the Church Board took up the issue for the first time. Two members had requested letters to take with them to the Jehovah's Witnesses and the Moravian Church, respectively. The Board discussed the matter, but voted to terminate the two members' letters and make no change in the congregation's policy.

In March 1946 another case came to the Official Board. Richard Myer requested a letter to transfer his membership. The minutes report, "The question of granting letters to those joining other denominations was discussed at length." At the March 20, 1946, Council Meeting, "The church voted to grant a letter to Richard Myer, who wishes to join the Lutheran Church of Brickerville."

Five years later the congregation took a much larger step toward respecting other denominations, when it adopted open communion. Until 1951 the Lititz Brethren practiced close communion: Only Brethren in good standing could take part in the love feast. So some non-members, who attended regularly, were active, and in some cases even held church offices, could not commune. That changed September 12, 1951, when the congregation voted 42-12 to adopt open communion. All Christians now could participate. The change came almost immediately after a decision at the 1951 Annual Conference recommending "that local churches, where they so desire, may extend to evangelical Christians the privilege of participating in the Love Feast."

Not long after the arrival of Pastor Dick the piano finally completed its long journey to the church sanctuary. In January 1946 Council approved the use of a piano in the "auditorium" for a choir cantata. The September 1947 Council accepted the gift of a piano from the Crusaders Class "for use on special occasions." Verna (Schlosser) Sollenberger, who began as choir director in October 1947, remembered that the choir still sang *a cappella* for the most part during her time as director. Sometimes pieces that were intended to be accompanied were adapted and sung *a cappella*. The piano was used for rehearsals. Gradually the choir began to sing with piano accompaniment.

According to Landis Stehman, at one point the piano was kept in a room outside the sanctuary and was moved in only when the choir was to sing a song with accompaniment. "Al Keller was janitor at the time," Landis recalled, "and we had the piano out in the side room there. He'd be pushing this thing in and out. When the choir didn't use it, well, then we had to push the piano out. Al said he was getting tired of doing that and we should either leave the piano in or out. So we left it in."

In November 1945 the church hired Albert Ebbert as full-time music director. Ebbert, who was Lutheran, directed the senior choir and the newly formed junior choir. While Ralph Gonder had received nominal pay for directing the male chorus years earlier, Ebbert appears to have been the church's first salaried music professional. Previous choir and chorus directors were Harvey Eberly, who in the early years of the church often led singing schools, and Gonder. Verna Sollenberger served as choir director from October 1947 until April 1950.

In 1946 the church received a $100 donation to establish an organ fund. Apparently the fund grew over the next few years. In 1949 the Improvement Committee was given the go-ahead to make plans to install the congregation's first organ in the sanctuary. The Mohler pipe organ, which was dedicated April 29, 1951, cost $5,131. B. Garis Daniels was the first organist and also directed the choir from November 1950 until 1955. The new organ introduced one of the few changes in worship during the Jacob Dick years—the addition of an organ prelude. The January 1951 Council approved the purchase of choir gowns, when funds became available.

Members described the Jacob Dick years as a positive time in the life of the church. The young pastor devoted much energy to working with youth. He also helped intensify the congregation's interest in Brethren Service relief work during the post-war period.

The February 17, 1946, issue of the *Lititz Messenger* listed 26 young people who recently had been discharged from the military. As those people came home, the Lititz church was sending out "sea-going cowboys," who accompanied shipments of heifers to Europe. Among the Lititz sea-going cowboys were Levi Weaver, Stanley Schoenberger, Richard Waltz, Jean de Perrot, Harry Badorf Jr., James Dietrich, Kenneth Dietrich, Richard Nolt, Milton Jurrell, Richard Wenger, Ken-

Members of the choir sing in the Center Street church around 1955. The congregation approved the purchase of its first choir gowns at the January 1951 Council Meeting.

neth Gibble, and Clair Becker. Pastor Dick, himself, spent a three-month sabbatical in Europe during the summer of 1947. Kenneth Frantz served as summer pastor during that time.

Notable speakers came to Lititz to speak about the ongoing relief efforts. In March 1948 Ben Bushong, Material Aid Director of the Brethren Service Commission, spoke at Lititz. In May it was David Hanawalt, State Director of Overseas Relief. In 1949 Juniata College president Calvert N. Ellis spent a day at Lititz, talking about a World Council of Churches meeting and European relief work. Notable revival speakers during the Dick years were Charles C. Ellis, former president of Juniata College and Annual Conference moderator; Rufus D. Bowman, president of Bethany Biblical Seminary; *Gospel Messenger* editor Desmond Bittinger; and Harry K. Zeller, chairman of the General Brotherhood Board.

The Lititz church also supported China missionaries Delores Hartman Snader and Mrs. Paul Hoover during these years and invited returning missionaries to speak, including Dr. and Mrs. Roy Pfaltzgraff, pioneers in treatment of leprosy in Nigeria. The congregation sponsored mission events such as its School of Missions, one of which lasted for five Sundays in February and March 1951. For many years the congregation invited missionaries to speak at a special candle lighting service during the Christmas season.

Earl Bowman: Better Slow Than Rash

Pastor Dick resigned at the March 12, 1952, Council Meeting. The congregation held a farewell covered dish for the Dicks at the end of May, before they went to Europe for a three-year Brethren Service assignment in Kassel, Germany.

Lowell Zuck served as interim pastor during the summer of 1952. Earl and Leah Bowman arrived from the Harrisonburg (Va.) church in August 1952.

Pastor Bowman's stay at Lititz was brief—less than three years. Much more formal than Pastor Dick, Pastor Bowman was the first Lititz minister to wear a robe while preaching. A formal goal-setting process began with Pastor Bowman, when in 1953 he submitted 11 goals for the congregation's approval.

The January 14, 1953, Council approved the beginning of regular membership classes. Again, the initiative came from Pastor Bowman, who wished to conduct membership classes among the children and youth. This decision marked a departure from the past and likely played a role in the disappearance of regular revival services in the early 1960s. During the first 40 years of the congregation's life, most new members were brought into the congregation through revival meetings. Guest evangelists would preach at a one-week- or two-weeks-long series of meetings. Invitations were extended to those who wished to come forward at the end of each service, accept Christ, and join the church. After revival meetings, the new converts received instruction and were baptized.

The initiation of regular membership classes changed how members came into the church. Instruction on membership was now given before young people had made a decision for Christ and the church. Gradually, membership classes came to play the role that revival meetings had played. So, though Pastor Bowman's time in Lititz was short, he implemented change that had lasting effects.

In his autobiography, *An Unknown Parson*, Pastor Bowman attributes his early exit to his own impatience.

Even before his arrival the congregation had discussed its space problems and tentatively approved plans to add on to the church. When Pastor Bowman arrived in 1952, membership stood at just under 500. He felt that adding on was only a stop-gap measure that would aggravate present parking problems. He urged moving to a new location and grew impatient when the congregation balked at his suggestion.

He wrote, "So I became a bit restless. For I could not see much of anything happening. To me it looked too much like maintaining the 'status quo.' Even the most capable of leaders of the Lititz Church at that time seemed too cautious and timid and slow in arriving at decisions which, any way one looked at it, were worthy."

He recognized his impatience a few years later when the congregation did erect a new building. He wrote that he had forgotten "an old bit of wisdom that 'all things come to those who wait.' One quality I have observed about the people of the Lititz Church which is a commendable asset: they cannot be rushed into anything, but once they have made up their minds and chartered [sic] their course there is no turning back. . . ; and while they may seem to move slowly, yet this may be much wiser than to be rash, and in due time they will arrive at a worthy objective." He concluded, "I feel we made a mistake in leaving Lititz and I should have demonstrated more patience."

Pastor Bowman announced his resignation at the October 20, 1954, Council, and left at the end of that year to become pastor of the Mack Memorial Church of the Brethren in Dayton, Ohio. G. Wayne Glick, Assistant Professor of Religion at Franklin and Marshall College, served as a supply preacher at Lititz, beginning January 1, 1955.

Floyd McDowell: "Behold, I Make All Things New"

E. Floyd McDowell was installed as the new pastor on April 3, 1955. McDowell and his wife, Lois, came to Lititz from the Palmyra (Pa.) congregation, where Floyd served as assistant pastor. McDowell's hobby was flying, and when the 27-year-old pastor landed in Lititz he hit the ground running. A flurry of significant changes began almost as soon as McDowell climbed from the cockpit to begin his first solo pastorate.

In August 1955 the congregation voted to adopt a new plan of organization. From the congregation's beginning, power had been centered primarily in the Official Board, which was comprised of deacons and ministers. Thus, in addition to their responsibilities in spiritual nurture, the deacons and ministers also were the primary administrative unit of the church. Prior to McDowell's arrival the congregation had appointed a committee to consider reorganization. With the coming of a new pastor, the committee wondered if it might not be wise to postpone reorganization until McDowell came on board. "My counsel," said Floyd in a 1989 interview, "was 'No, let's just move ahead with it, then we can all start fresh.' And that's what we did." Franklin Cassel was the primary architect of the new plan, drawing from other church's plans. Annual Conference had recommended such organizational change prior to the Lititz decision.

Essentially, the new plan replaced the Official Board with a Board of Administration. The new Board was divided into seven five-member commissions: Christian Education, Ministry and Evangelism, Missions and Service, Music and Worship, Properties and Finance, Fellowship and Recreation, and Spiritual Nurture. The deacons and ministers comprised the Spiritual Nurture Commission. The old position of presiding elder

Adults and children at a Vacation Bible School in the late 1950s. In the adult picture, Pastor Floyd McDowell is at right. In the children's picture teacher Verna (Weaver) Moseman is at right.

was replaced with the moderator, a position open to the laity. The new plan also allowed for electing deacons to serve three-year terms, rather than for life. Term deacons were elected for the first time in April 1958. This plan of organization, with a few changes, served the congregation until 1986.

Floyd McDowell believes the change in organization paved the way for other key decisions in the second half of the 1950s. The new plan of organization transferred responsibility from the deacons and ministers to the rest of the congregation. Before the change, the Official Board apparently had a reputation for being conservative and perhaps wasn't moving fast enough for the congregation on some matters. "You had entrenched power," Floyd explained. "I think the church recognized that. Even the deacons recognized that. Some were reluctant to admit it, I suppose, but they recognized that it would be good to get other people involved."

Franklin Cassel believed the deacons "were resistant to the change because it meant, in their way of looking at it, sort of a demotion, an elimination of the authority and decision-making power that they had." While some of the deacons may have felt that way, Landis Stehman and Levi Weaver, both of whom were deacons at that time, said they supported the change. "I was much in favor of it," said Levi. "It made it better for the deacons, even though a lot of them were opposed to it."

Floyd observed that even those deacons who initially opposed the change later appreciated it and saw the merit of sharing the work of the church with more people. And he added, "The sharing of power was very key to what happened in the church during the next four or five years."

Opening Wide the "Lamb's Book of Life"

The most significant change to follow on the heels of the new organization had to do with membership requirements. From their beginning, the Lititz Brethren rejected all forms of baptism other than trine immersion. So when members of other denominations wished to join the Brethren, they had to submit themselves to a proper Brethren baptism.

During the late 1940s the Official Board dealt with a related issue: "the wisdom of having non-Brethren people hold offices of the local Sunday school." The minutes report, "Some were strongly opposed." Apparently they were a minority voice, however, because non-Brethren did hold offices in the Sunday school. In fact they participated actively in almost all aspects of the church's life. As Brethren continued to marry non-Brethren, the problem grew worse. By the time Pastor McDowell arrived, the church had a significant number of couples where one partner was a member and the other was not. Many, he said, came from Lutheran background. The non-members would not join because they did not want to be rebaptized. Many resented the implication that their former baptisms were invalid. In fact, said Floyd, the minister at the Lutheran church taught that it was wrong to be rebaptized.

Elwood and Pauline Gibble were an example of a couple facing this conundrum. "My wife was a United Brethren at the time," explained Elwood. "We got married in 1948. She was assistant Sunday school superintendent and taught Sunday school the whole time, but she couldn't be a member [without being rebaptized]. That was pretty difficult for me to swallow." Melvin Brubaker, a Mennonite, was serving as Sunday school superintendent.

A move was underway in the congregation during Earl Bowman's pastorate to accept people without rebaptism, according to Franklin Cassel, but the item didn't come to Council Meeting until April 1956, when a "Resolution on the Question of Rebaptism" was debated for an hour-and-a-half. The resolution stated:

> Whereas the local church through the years has sustained serious membership losses due to our own members joining the denomination of the spouse, and
>
> Whereas the local church has failed frequently to add prospective members because of the requirement of re-baptism, and
>
> Whereas the requirement of re-baptism represents a denial of the validity and religious experience of other groups, and
>
> Whereas in the Church of the Brethren nationally over half of its churches no longer require re-baptism,
>
> Be it resolved:
>
> 1. That the local church continue to teach and practice Trine Immersion as the historic initiatory rite of entrance into the church.
>
> 2. That in receiving into membership those from other evangelical bodies, if they are satisfied with the method of their previous baptism and if their manner of life indicates genuine religious experience, we accept such persons on their confession of faith.

After the debate the congregation agreed to continue to study the matter. It was brought to a vote at the October 1956 Council. The vote was 91-50 in favor, or 64%. Since a two-thirds majority was required to implement such a change the motion failed. Not until October 1958 did the congregation vote to accept members from other denominations without rebaptism, by a vote of 61-16. Even then the debate was heated. Many remember that one longtime member made an emotional speech in opposition to the change and slowly headed toward the door. Mayno Hershey described the scene: "Floyd McDowell jumped up. I'd give anything in the world to have what he said. He talked and this man just gradually came back very slowly and sat down." Floyd no longer remembered what he said, but he thinks the incident was a turning point in the debate. Sunday school superintendent Melvin Brubaker was the first member to be admitted under the new policy.

Accepting new members without rebaptism had been sanctioned in a statement on church extension at the 1958 Annual Conference that summer in Des Moines, Iowa. Lititz adopted the change just four months after the Conference decision, and had, in fact, tried to make the change two years before Annual Conference had spoken.

A number of other "firsts" took place between 1955 and 1959. The first issue of the *Lititz Observer* was published in 1956. In 1957 the church hired Mary Lou Thomas, their first church secretary. She worked part-time for a dollar an hour. The Cherub choir was organized later that year. Also, in October 1956, the congregation voted to buy a property at 371 E. Main Street to house the Botschoff family, refugees from Russia. This appears to be the first refugee family the congregation sponsored. During 1958 the congregation sponsored a student exchange, with Lititz member Peggy Coulson going to Germany and Dorothee Beyer coming to Lititz. During McDowell's pastorate the congregation also provided the first pastor's office in the church.

Mary Lou Thomas earned a dollar an hour as the church's first paid secretary.

WE WOULD BE BUILDING

When the congregation moved to their new church on Center Street in 1926, Margaret Krumbine remembered how enormous the new building seemed. Yet, just 20 years later, the Lititz church was outgrowing that building. A Church Improvement Committee met, beginning in the mid-1940s to discuss what could be done. Floyd recalled, "I walked into the midst of that situation where very soon I learned that they had been trying for a long, long time to [decide what to do about their space problems]. There was great diversity of thought."

With the change in organization in 1955 the new Board of Administration took on the responsibilities of the Church Improvement Committee. The space problem was growing more acute. According to Margaret Krumbine, "We were

THE CENTER STREET CHURCH

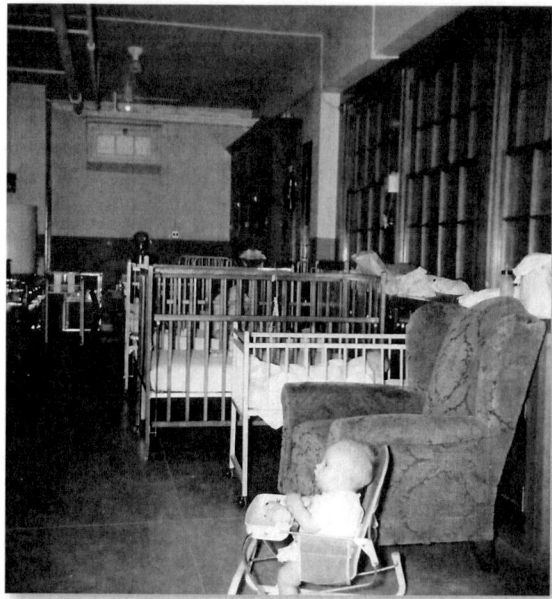

The church on Center Street (in center of top photo) was landlocked, making it difficult to expand. Inside, the kitchen doubled as a nursery as the church struggled to find space to accommodate a growing congregation.

falling all over each other in the basement trying to conduct Sunday school classes between the curtains." And the Sunday school was growing.

Initially, the congregation leaned toward adding onto the Center Street church. But without extra space for parking, an addition was not feasible. Things started moving ahead in January 1957 when the congregation gave the Board the go-ahead to search for a new site. The congregation had a pastor with the right skills for choosing building sites. Pastor McDowell, who served on the Lititz Planning Commission, examined several sites from his airplane and landed, convinced that the West Orange Street property, located on what would be a growing edge of Lititz, should be the site of the next Lititz Church of the Brethren.

In May a report was presented to Council based on the work of eight study committees. In July architect George Savage presented for consideration preliminary plans for a new church and for an addition to the present building. The drawings were based on projections of what the congregation's needs would be in 1967. Savage suggested that the church might want to consider building in units, with the first unit adequate to meet present needs.

Also in July the Board interviewed A. Wayne Carr, a Brethren minister from Manchester, Ind., and head of Carr and Associates, financial consultants. But the congregation wasn't ready to make a decision. So, at Pastor McDowell's urging, the Board called in one more consultant, Dr. Charles Leach, editor of *Church Management* magazine. Dr. Leach came at the end of September. "He was kind of a genius," said Floyd. "We gave him all the information that we had, and he made a convincing case dollar-wise and otherwise that we really ought to move."

After some 15 years of discussion and planning, at a Council in November 1957, the Board brought a comprehensive proposal for consideration by the congregation. The proposal included a couple potentially controversial items. Specifically, the Board recommended: 1) Purchasing from the Lititz Moravian congregation eight to ten acres of land at an estimated cost of $14,000; 2) A new building as proposed by architect Savage; 3) The appointment of a special 16-member Building Committee; 4) The adoption of a unified budget and planned giving program; and 5) Employment of finance consultants Carr and Associates to spearhead a financial drive.

The proposal passed by a narrow 89-80 margin. It seems likely that the vote was close because so many measures were approved at one time. Different people objected to different parts of the plan. Not the least controversial was the decision to hire Carr and Associates, professionals from outside the congregation, to lead the financial campaign. "We knew that was going to raise a lot of static," Floyd remembered. But the measure passed and the Carrs led a successful financial campaign.

Floyd believes that the unified budget was reasonably well received. Previously the congregation gave many offerings earmarked for specific destinations. "The notion was that people would get a better sense of their stewardship if they could see this lump sum as opposed to fracturing it into all these different offerings," Floyd explained.

The unified budget also spelled an end to many fundraising projects. One of the most popular of such projects was making *fasnachts* each year on Shrove Tuesday. The women of the church would work almost around the clock for two days, baking as many as 2,000 dozen of the doughy delights to sell throughout the community. Mary Weaver and others highlighted the rich fellowship that went along with making *fasnachts*. According to Landis Stehman, "The sanctuary would smell a couple Sundays afterward."

The November 1957 Council decisions paved the way to begin negotiations to buy 8.55 acres of land, to develop detailed building plans, and to get the financial campaign underway. In December 1958 the congregation agreed to begin building in spring 1962. In January they approved a number of stop-gap measures to make more Sunday school space at the Center Street church. Even those measures proved inadequate, so the congregation decided to begin building in 1961.

With plans for the new church firmly in place, Pastor McDowell resigned April 12, 1959, and left September 1, to become Director of Development at Bethany Theological Seminary. He led the Lititz congregation less than five years, but during his brief pastorate the congregation made key decisions that have had lasting effects.

CHAPTER 4

The Orange Street Era:
NEW BUILDING, NEW MINISTRIES

The congregation elected Olden Mitchell pastor in June 1959. He and his wife, Myrtle Belle, arrived in September. Members remember Mitchell as the hardest working pastor they ever had. He routinely put in long hours, but he maintained he never failed to take a full day or two half days off each week and was always available to his family. (The 75th anniversary history stated that Mitchell routinely put in 80-hour weeks, which he rebutted in a letter.) Franklin Cassel noted that Pastor Mitchell's aggressive style was instrumental in getting the new organizational plan (adopted in 1955) to work well. He held people accountable and didn't hesitate to tell them what he thought they should be doing.

While major decisions regarding the church building project had been made, the congregation still had a new church to build after Pastor Mitchell's arrival. Bids were opened May 31, 1961. Of the eight builders submitting bids, William Murry and Sons, Inc., of Lancaster, was lowest at $290,958. Construction began in June 1961 and by June

76   A CENTURY OF MINISTRY, A FUTURE OF PROMISE

The steeple on the new church on Orange Street wasn't yet in place for the June 17, 1962, building dedication. Participants in Vacation Bible School were treated to a show when the steeple was lifted into place on August 16, 1962.

1962 was complete enough to move in. The new church was dedicated June 14-17, 1962. The steeple was not yet in place at the time of dedication.

The Lititz Brethren received $50,000 from the Church of God for the Center Street property and parsonage. In late May 1962 the Brethren purchased a new parsonage at 117 Mayfield Drive on Kissel Hill. All told, the cost for the entire building project was $425,112.43. The land, church

The new church building on Orange Street was surrounded by fields when it was built across from the new high school in 1962. The congregation rightly discerned that before long their new church would be part of a growing edge of Lititz.

building, and furnishings accounted for $406,349.52, and the new parsonage cost $18,762.91. The new building did not include the chapel or the large fellowship hall, both of which were provided for in the original plan and were added later, as architect Savage had suggested. In a 1964 Council report, Pastor Mitchell said that "our denominational church building counselor has described our building as possibly the most adequate total church plant in the Brotherhood." He reported that more than 50 churches had sent representatives of their Building Committees to examine the Lititz church.

The new church left the congregation with a debt of $179,300. Twice during the early 1960s Council voted against hiring a professional outsider to help raise funds to pay off the debt. In 1966, however, all the congregation's debt problems were solved, thanks to a gift of about $291,000 from the Daniel and Ella Withers' estate. In *An Unknown Parson,* Earl Bowman takes credit for this gift. Daniel Withers had become a millionaire in the tobacco business. He was a member of the Lutheran church and his wife a member of the Church of the Brethren. He apparently respected Pastor Bowman, who suggested that in his will he divide his estate between an area college, a hospital, his own church, his wife's church, and his nieces and nephews. Withers died years after Pastor Bowman left Lititz, but the estate was divided approximately as he had suggested.

In a letter dated May 15, 1990, following publication of the 75th anniversary history, Olden Mitchell offered an alternative view of who was primarily responsible for the Withers bequest:

"(Pastor Bowman) may have had some influence on the final decision," Mitchell wrote, "but Mrs. Withers gave the

More than 50 church building committees sent representatives to examine the new, state-of-the-art "church plant." The building cost $406,349, which was quickly paid, thanks to a generous bequest from the Daniel and Ella Withers' estate.

credit entirely to John G. Hershey; and he (Hershey), on more than one occasion, shared in my presence how he had worked on this with Mr. Withers. Mr. Withers gave his estate to six causes or agencies, and Mrs. Withers gave all her estate to the Lititz Church."

With the Withers money, the congregation liquidated its remaining $162,000 debt and divided $30,000 among a number of worthy institutions. The rest was invested in U.S. government securities and bank saving certificates.

New Church, New Steeple, But Where Are the People?

Ironically, shortly after the congregation moved into its new facility, capable of accommodating a large Sunday school, Sunday school attendance started to decline. Sunday school attendance peaked from 1960 to 1962, nearly reaching 400 each of those years, and then began a marked decline that has continued with few interruptions.

Shortly after Pastor Mitchell's arrival, the congregation also approved creating a new inactive members' list. Re-activating inactive members became a top priority during Mitchell's pastorate, and the Under Shepherd Program that got underway in 1961 was at the heart of that plan. In an October 1959 report he wrote, "There is no such thing as an inactive Christian! Ways must be found to revive and restore to Christ and the church all our inactive members. . . ."

In October 1959 the Lititz church consisted of 568 members. Average attendance was 318. Mitchell had calculated that approximately 260 of those attending were members. In the same report he wrote, "It is a spiritual tragedy that half of our members miss the experience of worship on Sunday morning." Church attendance did improve over the next few years, but since 1970 average attendance at the Lititz church typically has been less than half of its total membership.

A related concern was Council Meeting attendance, which had been dwindling over the years. In September 1961 the Board approved a number of measures to shore up attendance, but they proved ineffective. The low attendance of 41 at the May 1964 Council led to a discussion of the necessity of having a quorum to conduct business. In September the congregation voted to rescind that part of the organizational plan calling for a 10 percent quorum of members at Council.

Olden Mitchell: Ministering the Bread and Cup

New pastors bring changes in church life, and Pastor Mitchell was no exception. On Maundy Thursday 1962, the congregation held its first bread and cup communion service. About 260 attended. In 1964 a second bread and cup communion was added to the church schedule. Since then the congregation has continued to observe both the full love feast and the bread and cup communion twice a year.

Following the opening of membership in 1958, the congregation had taken in many members from churches who observed communion more often than twice a year. These members, many of whom were raised with a different understanding of communion, likely felt the need for more frequent observances. At the same time, noted Franklin Cassel, there were some people who did not want to wash feet. The bread and cup communion gave those people opportunity to commune.

As Harry Badorf remembered it, the decision initiating the bread and cup communion wasn't particularly controversial. But, he said, "I think there was concern that we might not have as good an attendance at the regular love feasts." Statistics seemed to bear that out. Average love feast attendance peaked at 426 in 1962, the year the first bread and cup communion was held. It declined steadily to 320 in 1975, rebounded briefly, and then continued its decline. Average love feast attendance in 1988 increased to 294. Membership stood at 776. In 2013 love feast attendance averaged less than 200 out of about 624 active members.

The early 1960s also marked the end of regular revival services, or evangelistic meetings. Up until 1959 the congregation had regular week-long evangelistic meetings at least once a year. It appears that 1959 was the last regular week-long revival service. Since then the congregation has, from time to time, held shorter series of meetings, but week-long revival services are a thing of the past. At the same time, the end of evangelistic meetings did not necessarily signal the end of evangelistic fervor. In 1960 the congregation created a separate Evangelism Commission, and "Evangelism and Enlistment" were major goals for the 1961-62 church year. In 1979 many members supported the Leighton-Ford crusade in their area. The congregation would embark on the three-year Passing on the Promise program in 1988, expressing a renewed interest in evangelism.

While some traditional Brethren practices were declining in the early 1960s, the congregation was turning toward the community and speaking out on the social issues of the day. In September 1963, in the midst of the nation's racial turmoil, the Council reaffirmed that anyone can be a member of the congregation, regardless of race, and authorized the Mission and Service Commission to study and propose ways to involve the church in "appropriate forms of reconciliation in the present racial crisis." One such activity was a pulpit exchange with an African American congregation in Lancaster. Members also were encouraged to write letters supporting the Civil Rights bill, and six Lititz families hosted African American children for a week during the summer. The congregation also sponsored an African American child to attend Camp Swatara.

In 1963 Lititz Brethren organized a Cub Scout pack, and

SCOUTING IN A PEACE CHURCH

The formation of Cub and Boy Scout troops in 1963 and 1964 was the beginning of a lasting relationship between the congregation and the Scouts. Boy Scout Troop #154 was officially chartered in 1965, with Tom W. Williams serving as Scoutmaster and Eugene B. Ludwig as Assistant. Charter Scouts included Chester Coen, Tom Ludwig, and Terry Zeiders. A February 1991 *Observer* article noted that in its first 25 years, the troop had "guided hundreds of boys in building character, fostering citizenship and developing mental, moral and physical fitness." During that time the troop had produced 12 Eagle Scouts. Henry R. Gibbel was listed as the leader in 1991. For a time the congregation also sponsored as many as four Girl Scout and Brownie Troops, who met at the church in a room set aside for use by scouts. The February 2010 *Observer* noted that Troop 154 would celebrate 100 years of scouting and 45 years of association with the church on February 7.

Along with being big supporters of scouting, the Lititz congregation also has been active in advocating for peace. While there's nothing inherently incompatible between the stated objectives of the Boy Scouts of America and a peace church, the two do embrace potentially conflicting views of patriotism. The uniforms, pledging allegiance to the flag, and "do my duty to God and country" portion of the Scout Oath can be off-putting to conscientious objectors to war, and pacifism would not be embraced by the vast majority of scouts. Somehow the Lititz Brethren have managed to make peace with scouting, while also maintaining commitments of a historic peace church.

the following year a Boy Scout troop, beginning a decades-long partnership between the congregation and scouting.

In 1964 the church hired its first assistant pastor; D. Howard Keiper began in September 1964 as part-time Minister of Visitation. In July 1965 a dedication service was held for the church's newly built pavilion. J. Madison Deitrich provided the impetus and donated many of the materials for this project, and the pavilion continues in use 50 years later.

In March 1966 Pastor Mitchell announced his resignation, effective in August. He accepted a call from the Lincolnshire congregation, in Fort Wayne, Ind. In a report to the Board, he cited a number of practical reasons for his resignation, but perhaps the most telling was the church's attitude toward change. At a meeting of the Ministry Commission and the Board with the district executive, the feeling was expressed that the congregation was ready to slow down after 10 years of rapid change. They urged the pastor to avoid further changes and to give the congregation a chance to catch its breath. Pastor Mitchell felt that the congregation needed to continue to push ahead to remain faithful to its calling. There was no time for sitting back.

CLEM ROSENBERGER: A TURN TOWARD THE COMMUNITY

The congregation elected W. Clemens Rosenberger to be their new pastor on May 4, 1966. Clem and Margaret arrived from the Westmont congregation, in Johnstown, in September, and stayed longer than the previous three pastors combined. Rosenberger's 16 years were marked by more building and increased community involvement.

> ### I WON'T SLOW DOWN
>
> Pastor Mitchell didn't slow down for a long time. He was in his mid-fifties when he moved on from Lititz, but served additional pastorates and interim pastorates. All told, he pastored for more than 70 years and was a frequent letter writer to the Church of the Brethren magazine *Messenger* into his late 90s, sometimes championing progressive causes. He died at Timbercrest Retirement Community in North Manchester, Indiana, on September 8, 2013, a week shy of his 101st birthday. Though he died as a centenarian, his wasn't the longest life of his five siblings. His brother, Dr. S. Earl Mitchell died in 2011 at age 101.

In May 1967 the congregation voted to find a more adequate parsonage and to explore church expansion. Members felt it was time to build the large fellowship hall that had been part of the architect's original plans. Since the congregation had moved into the new church, some members were dissatisfied with the way the love feast was conducted. Interestingly, "the most adequate church plant in the whole denomination" had inadequate space for love feast. Not everyone could fit in the small fellowship hall. The alternatives were holding love feast in two shifts or holding it in the sanctuary, which would necessitate having a simpler meal—a sandwich. Love feast without the traditional beef-rice soup just didn't seem like love feast to some.

In March 1968 the congregation voted 77-14 to expand. The addition would include a fellowship hall/gymnasium, a kitchen, youth room, scout room, and storage space. The old fellowship hall would be converted into five classrooms. At the same meeting, plans for the memorial chapel were unanimously approved. Members of the Gibbel family wished to donate

86   A CENTURY OF MINISTRY, A FUTURE OF PROMISE

The church as it looked after the dedication of a fellowship hall/gymnasium, kitchen, scout room, and chapel on September 14, 1969. The church pavilion also had been added in 1965. New facilities contributed to growth in community ministries.

the chapel to the church in honor of their grandmother, Florence Gibbel, and in memory of grandfather Henry R. Gibbel and parents Henry B. and Lois H. Gibbel.

In May it was agreed to buy a lot in the nearby Becker development to build a new parsonage. In June the bids of builders Don Kepner and Abram S. Horst were accepted for the parsonage and church building projects, respectively. The parsonage on the corner of Woodland and Becker was completed the following spring, and the fellowship hall and chapel were dedicated September 14, 1969. The new gym and Pastor Rosenberger's easygoing style helped to open the church to more community involvement.

"I was kind of a town cleric," Clem recalls. "I loved to go downtown and have coffee—that nickel coffee at Benner's—and walk the streets. I developed a lot of non-Brethren friends in town. In the course of that, I think the church developed more of an image of being for the town and for the people."

"Clem was loved by the community," said Jim Gibbel. "He knew people all through the community. His way of making people feel welcome, along with the fellowship hall, really opened up the church to the community."

The congregation's expanded facilities enabled it to participate in a number of outreach ministries. In 1967 a Youth Club for middle school-age youth was begun. (It later included upper elementary-age kids, as well.) Clem, who had begun a similar program during his previous pastorate, says the Youth

A LASTING IMPRINT

Not only did Youth Club encourage youth in their faith walk and bring some new families into the church, it also contributed to the creation of a unique enterprise within the church that continues today. One of the early service components of Youth Club was instruction in printing. Charles Forry, a Lititz member who owned a printing business, donated some excess equipment and set up a print shop in the former church kitchen. For decades he taught teens how to set type and run the presses. Kids helped print items such as banquet tickets, small jobs for the Meals on Wheels program, a love feast songbook, and other jobs for the church.

Charlie printed some of the regular larger jobs, such as church bulletins and newsletters, at Forry & Hacker until his retirement in 1983, but for nearly two decades after that he oversaw a team of volunteers that met nearly all of the Lititz church's printing needs, while also doing some paying jobs for outside customers. Proceeds from outside print jobs supported the Youth Club program. Printing was discontinued as part of Youth Club in the mid-1990s, and Charlie retired from the print shop early in 2001. He was recognized during a February 4, 2001, worship service for the lasting imprint that he left on youth and on the church by volunteering his time and talents.

After Charlie's retirement, the presses rolled on under the direction of Harry Badorf and assistant Gerry Kurl. Carl Martin eventually took Harry's place, and today Gerry and Carl are listed among the staff as "church printers." A framed picture of Charlie and Harry has hung on the print shop wall since 2010, paying tribute to the pioneer printers of the Lititz congregation.

Charles Forry, shown here around 1980 with "apprentice" Mike DeSilva, taught printing as part of Youth Club for many years. The print shop that he began in the church continues today under the leadership of Gerald Kurl and Carl Martin.

Club "gave us some evangelistic penetration into the community." The program included time for recreation, Bible study, a meal, and a service hour. He recalled that in its early years, Youth Club may have had 50 or more junior high youth, a third of whom were not from within the congregation. The Youth Club program would evolve and continue for more than 30 years, before giving way to a new midweek program for all ages in 2000.

In 1973 the congregation began cooperation with Intermediate Unit 13, renting five classrooms. Eventually IU 13 used the entire educational wing, before moving into its own facilities. Also in 1973 the Lititz congregation helped establish a Meals on Wheels program in Lititz.

For a number of years Warwick Middle School students came to the Lititz church for instruction in the time-release program. Linden Hall and the Lititz Christian School have used the gym, and for nearly 20 years the Warwick Association of Churches sponsored a special education class, held Sunday mornings at the Lititz church. Many other groups began using the church fellowship hall—even an aerobics group! In 1973 the Lititz congregation played a role in creating a Brethren Volunteer Service project at the Lititz Community Center, and Lititz members hosted BVSers.

International Contacts

During the Rosenberger years, the congregation had a number of international contacts through student exchanges, sponsoring refugees, a pastoral exchange, and a unique mission exchange involving the Bitrus Sawa family.

In cooperation with the Foreign Missions Commission of the General Brotherhood Board, in 1967 the Lititz congregation hosted Nigerian Brethren Bitrus Sawa and his family. Bitrus needed a master's degree in order to take a position at the Waka (Nigeria) school, according to Franklin Cassel, who chaired the Lititz Missions and Service Commission when the Sawas were in Lititz. The denomination paid for the Sawas' transportation to and from the U.S., and the Lititz church provided housing and care for the family.

Bitrus earned his master's in education, taking courses first at Penn State and then Millersville State College. The Sawas also spoke to more than 30 groups. Franklin and Margaret Cassel provided a second-hand car, and the church provided housing. "We were very happy to share in [sponsoring the Sawas]," said Franklin. "It was a good experience for the congregation. A lot of good friendships were made." Bitrus and family returned to Nigeria in September 1968.

In 1969 the congregation sent Lititz member Dale Shenk to the Federal Republic of Germany and hosted exchange student Ellen Heimer. During the 1970s and 1980s the Lititz church sponsored a number of refugee families. Included were the Vermani family from Uganda, settled in 1972; the Konsynonth family, who were resettled during the 1980s; three brothers from Vietnam; two women from eastern Europe; and additional families from southeast Asia. Somphop Kongsynonth and his wife, Sara, are members of the church today.

A rather unique exchange came about as a result of Pastor Rosenberger's sabbatical in 1974. After spending time in the Middle East and Europe, Rosenberger studied eight weeks in England as part of the British-American Pulpit Exchange. Later the Lititz church hosted two ministers from England.

Beginnings of Successful Team Ministry

As church membership neared the 700 mark in the late 1960s the congregation saw the need for additional staff. In May 1968, D. Howard Keiper announced that he intended to resign. The congregation voted to hire Arlin G. Claassen as full-time associate pastor. Arlin and his wife, Helen, arrived in June 1969 from the McPherson (Kan.) Mennonite church. His primary responsibilities at Lititz were in Christian education, worship and music, and fellowship and recreation. Pastor Keiper was retained to do 10 hours of visitation per week and was named pastor emeritus in 1970 in appreciation for his years of service.

Pastors Rosenberger and Claassen worked well together as a team during Claassen's eight-and-a-half years, the first of a series of effective teams. Ernest Shenk pointed out that Lititz has been very fortunate in having successful team ministries. "For some reason pastors have been able to work well together here," he said. And that trend would continue with future long-serving teams. Claassen resigned June 19, 1978, to accept the pastorate of the Ivester (Iowa) congregation, and Ralph Z. Moyer began as the new associate in July 1980. When Pastor Claassen resigned, the congregation sold the Mayfield Drive parsonage and purchased a home on Second Avenue, across the street from the church. Robert Life served as a student intern from Bethany Theological Seminary during 1978 and 1979. Pastor Moyer continued the strong leadership in team ministry with Pastor Rosenberger.

The Rosenberger years (1966-1982) were calm in comparison to the flurry of changes in congregational life that had taken place under Pastors McDowell and Mitchell. But one subtle change did take place during the late 1960s

A PRECIPITATING EVENT

After reading about the disappearance of prayer coverings in the 75th anniversary history of the Lititz congregation, Pastor Mitchell shared what he felt was a precipitating event that took place at the October 1, 1961, love feast. A female member of the congregation came to the tables wearing a hat, instead of the traditional white covering expected by the church. A conscientious deaconess quietly confronted the hat-wearer and encouraged her to exchange her hat for a covering, causing some discomfort for both.

Following this incident, the deaconess asked the Spiritual Nurture Commission to clarify the church's position on women wearing coverings at love feast. Pastor Mitchell was asked to prepare "a white paper" as background for discussion at the next meeting, which he did. The paper largely dismissed the traditional covering as a cultural artifact and left little doubt where the pastor stood on the matter. The concluding paragraph stated, "Many minds are closed on some points cherished by them, not open to the truth—and the Holy Spirit would have difficulty in giving them new light if it differed from what they already knew. Jesus continually had to face this problem with the Pharisees and others who were very devout, but whose minds were closed to the truth."

Given the choice between being Pharisaical and Spirit-led, the commission, in Mitchell's words, "decided almost unanimously to allow each woman to decide whether to wear the covering, or any head covering, at the love feast services."

A member of the congregation with traditional leanings recalls that Pastor Mitchell "did much teaching to discourage the women in the church from wearing prayer coverings to worship." By 1989 only about one percent of the congregation's women wore a prayer covering to church on Sunday morning. A few more wore coverings to love feast. By 2014, the covering had virtually disappeared.

and early 1970s—the prayer covering virtually disappeared. Women such as Mary Weaver, Beatrice Mohler, and Margaret Krumbine remembered that the majority of women still wore prayer coverings to church well into the 1960s. The practice began a noticeable decline during Olden Mitchell's pastorate and all but disappeared in the late 1960s or early 1970s.

More controversial during these years was the decision to upgrade and expand the church organ. As early as January 1968 the congregation consulted with Carl Shull, accomplished organist and professor of music at Elizabethtown College. Shull recommended $34,000 be spent to make the Mohler organ that had been brought from the Center Street church adequate for the new facility. The congregation balked, decided to table the matter, and search for a cheaper way.

By the time the issue came to a vote in May 1979, similar repairs and expansion cost nearly $54,000. The congregation voted 53-34 to make the necessary changes, keeping the same console, but increasing the ranks from four to fifteen. But in July 1979, when the financing plans were discussed, disagreement surfaced. The church was nearly $14,000 behind its budget at the time. After an hour-and-a-half of discussion the congregation voted 44-42 to approve the contract for the organ improvements. The following year the concern over finances was shown to be unnecessary; the church received a $60,000 bequest from the Roy Walter estate. Ten percent of those funds were used for outreach and the rest to pay for the organ improvements. The revamped organ was dedicated May 3, 1981. The congregation also received several other bequests during the Rosenberger years.

Charismatic Controversy

Though the organ issue stirred the passion of some members, a far more significant issue was bubbling under the surface of the congregational life. A battle for the congregation's identity was being waged. Elwood Gibble was Board chair in the mid-1970s, when a group within the church was attracted to the charismatic movement. "These people were very critical of the leadership of the church," Elwood said. They desired a more charismatic style of worship and a more "spiritual" church. A number of outside speakers came into the area and further stirred the charismatic coals, among them Russell Bixler, the pastor of the Pittsburgh Church of the Brethren, who was a leader in the movement and author of the book *It Can Happen to Anybody*. Ultimately, many left during the 1980s. Although the loss of members was serious, Elwood Gibble suggested in 1989 that things could have been far worse without the reconciling skills of Pastor Rosenberger. Members describe Rosenberger as a peacemaker and a healer. "Clem took a lot of heat," said Elwood, "but he rode it out and tried to get through without a lot of controversy."

Clem Rosenberger accepted the call from the La Verne, California, congregation in January 1982 and completed his service at Lititz on June 30, after 16 years as pastor. During that time membership grew from 640 to 793 and the budget expanded from $66,000 to $220,000. That same year Kitty Grove resigned after 21 years as church secretary; Bonnie Hutchinson replaced her.

CHAPTER 5

Jimmy and Ralph:
THE 1980s AND 1990s

Jimmy R. Ross wasn't looking for a new church when he was asked to consider serving at Lititz, but he believed it was important to remain open to God's calling. He was in the midst of a satisfying 13-year-long pastorate at the Codorus congregation, located near Dallastown, Pa., and fully intended to continue there for many more years. What's more, he was in the final year of a Doctor of Ministry program and didn't need any distractions. "We were not eager to leave Codorus," Jimmy recalls, "and this call just sort of came out of the blue." But Jimmy and his wife, Betty, agreed to talk with the Lititz Search Committee, and they came to understand it as God's calling. Jimmy was named pastor in May 1983, and he and Betty arrived October 1. During the interim Howard Bernhard was hired to carry out visitation ministry, but he died shortly after he began.

A Pastor First

When Pastor Ross arrived on the scene in 1983, the congregation still hadn't fully resolved its differences over charismatic worship and congregational identity, which is one of the reasons Jimmy believes the congregation called him. He was a pastor first, who based his ministry on caring for people, and was recognized as a good people person and reconciler. "I think one of my gifts is pastoral care and being pastorally concerned about the people and the congregation," says Jimmy. "And that's also true for Ralph (Moyer). The basis of our ministry is pastoral care. We are more than anything else pastors. We preach, but we're pastors. And I think that's what Lititz was looking for."

Uncertainty created by the charismatic debate persisted and discussions continued until a Special Council Meeting was called in December 1985. The 161 members who attended approved a statement from the Board that reaffirmed the congregation's Brethren identity and voiced support for the leaders and programs of the church.

> *We affirm that the Lititz Congregation is a Church of the Brethren. We intend to remain faithful to Jesus Christ and to the doctrine, beliefs, and policies of the Church of the Brethren as we understand them. We support the pastors, the ministry, and the programs of the Lititz Church of the Brethren.*

Members interviewed in 1989 credited Pastor Ross for his skillful handling of the issue, but the congregation felt the effects of the charismatic exodus for years to come. Not everyone agrees on exactly how many people left, but a reasonable estimate seems to be around 35 members, along with their children. Most of those who left had been active workers in the church. A few returned some years later.

Another Successful Team

Pastors Ross and Moyer quickly formed a strong team, continuing a pattern that had begun in the 1970s with Clem Rosenberger and Arlin Claassen and carried on with Clem and Ralph. It didn't hurt that Jimmy and Ralph already were well acquainted. They had known each other for more than two decades and participated in the same pastoral support group during the 1970s, when Ralph had served at the York First Church of the Brethren and Jimmy at Codorus. In fact, Jimmy credits Ralph with pointing the congregation toward him as a potential pastoral candidate, who would be a good fit for Lititz and a good colleague for Ralph. That turned out to be true on both counts as they would work together for the next 15 years. Both Jimmy and Ralph point to their successful partnership as a highlight of their time at Lititz. "Ralph had been here three years," Jimmy recalls, "and we didn't have to spend any time learning to trust each other. We have always trusted each other. So that was a big advantage."

Jimmy and Ralph's partnership was embodied in the structure of the staff. "We shared a common understanding of ministry as being shared, or a mutual ministry," says Jimmy. "Neither of us was really interested in a hierarchy. It took some discussion to come to that point with the Ministry Commission, because I think a lot of people wanted to see me as the senior pastor. I simply said I did not feel comfortable supervising Ralph Moyer. He was my age. We went to seminary together.

We had practically the same number of years of experience. And so we worked at it where each of us took responsibilities and each day we checked in with each other. We were in constant conversation."

Jimmy handled the bulk of the preaching (three Sundays for Jimmy, one for Ralph) and administration, they shared visitation, and Ralph worked in special ministries with youth, families, and outreach, and enjoyed teaching Sunday school. "It was a jack of all trades kind of thing," says Ralph of his job description. But each leader was able to focus on their areas of giftedness. Jimmy embraced administration, for example, while Ralph did what he needed to in that area. Ralph carried on Clem Rosenberger's legacy of community involvement, taking time to drink coffee with the locals at Bingeman's Restaurant, chairing the Warwick Community Chest Food Bank and the Lititz CROP Walk for a time.

In the Atlantic Northeast District, Ralph was heavily involved in the ministries of Camp Swatara, serving on its Board and providing leadership during summer camps. He was instrumental in beginning an annual Family Weekend Camp for Lititz Brethren at Camp Swatara, which at its peak attracted nearly 100 people of various ages for a time of worship, fellowship, and community building. "It was a great time for the congregation to be in a different setting," Ralph recalls. More than 30 years later All Church Family Weekend Camp continues each fall.

Perhaps the ministry that Ralph and his wife, Annette, were best known for were the annual Marriage Enrichment events that they led for Lititz Brethren and others. Ralph and Annette had received training prior to coming to Lititz and had led weekend retreats to strengthen marriages in various congregations and districts. Beginning in 1987, they began to lead an

Children at the 2013 All Church Weekend at Camp Swatara pose with some artwork they helped create.

annual Marriage Enrichment Weekend for Lititz members at the Bird-in-Hand Motor Inn. A March 1991 *Lititz Observer* article reported that approximately 26 couples in the congregation had completed an "M.E. Weekend Retreat," with many continuing to meet in bi-monthly support groups after the initial weekend. In addition, the congregation hosted annual or semi-annual marriage enrichment events—often a dinner with a speaker focusing on relationships. Initially these nights out were for those who had completed a weekend retreat, but eventually they opened up to all couples in the congregation. Ralph and Annette led annual retreats for Lititz members until the mid-1990s and continued to meet with support groups that grew out of the weekend events beyond that. One support group, says Ralph, continues to meet in 2014.

> ### A DUCK TALE
>
> While ducks are a common sight at Camp Swatara's lake, one wouldn't expect to see ducks at the Lititz church, which sits rather high and dry. But the September 1990 issue of the congregational newsletter, *The Observer*, told this duck tale:
>
>> For several years a mother duck hatched her eggs near the children's Sunday school wing. The last two or more years she flew into the church courtyard and layed (sic) and hatched the eggs. Many people have been interested in the duck family, and have watched the ducklings grow. The staff and members tried to figure out how to get them out to no avail. Finally, Ken Graybill opened the door from the courtyard to the gym, and behold, mother duck waddled her little ones, in duck style, into the gym, down the hallway, and out the back door to freedom.
>
> Evidently satisfied with the arrangement, Mother Duck returned the following year, and the tradition has continued most years since then, including 2014, when Mama Duck and family again made their exit from the courtyard through the fellowship hall.

The pastoral team expanded when Henry Renn came on board as half-time Pastor for Christian Nurture in 1989. Henry served in that role until 1994, working in the areas of Christian education and youth. He was replaced by Tracy Wenger Sadd in August 1994. Tracy served as three-fourths-time Pastor for Christian Nurture until Spring 1999. During her tenure, the Lititz ministry team was viewed by some as a model. "In fact," says Jimmy, "they referred to the Lititz staff as the 'Dream

Team,' which I think was a little exaggerated." Dream Team or not, the Lititz staff led an insight session at the 1996 Church of the Brethren Annual Conference in Cincinnati on the topic of "Multiple Staff Ministries in Congregations."

Another significant member joined the team in 1984. Joan Fyock began as Director of Music Ministries and provided leadership for the church's music programs for the next two decades, accompanied for a dozen of those years by organist Chris Oetama, who would resign in 1998 and be replaced in January 1999 by John Huber, who continues as church organist today.

More Deacons and Greater Commitment

The "ministry team" wasn't limited to salaried staff, but included deacons and other lay members, as well. But Pastor Ross was surprised to see how thin his deacon bench was when he arrived. He recalls returning home from his first deacon meeting and telling Betty, "You won't believe this, but this church only has 12 deacon teams." That was for a congregation of 781 members with a weekly worship attendance of 360.

The time was ripe to beef up the role of deacons, not only because of what was happening at Lititz, but also in the larger church, where deacon ministry was receiving renewed attention. The 1983 Annual Conference approved a statement on "The Office of Deacon," which called for a renewal of the caregiving role of deacons in congregations and spurred the creation of new resources to equip deacons to serve more effectively. During Pastor Ross' tenure, the Deacon Board was enlarged and regular training events for deacons were held using "Called to Caregiving" materials from the denomination. Deacons were assigned lists of members to care for, and assumed a larger role in visitation. At times pastors included deacons in anointing services. And, of course, deacons continued to carry traditional responsibilities related to love feast, communion, and baptism services. In a March 1991 newsletter column Pastor Ross highlighted the expanding role of deacons as a sign of growth in the congregation. He observed "the congregation is experiencing the fruit of having our deacons more directly involved in the spiritual nurture and care of its members."

The renewed emphasis on deacons also became intertwined with a significant organizational change. In 1986 the congregation approved a new organizational plan, the first since 1955. (Minor adaptations had been made in the former plan.) In the old plan, the church called people to serve on specific commissions that comprised the Church Board. The Spiritual Nurture Commission was comprised of deacons. The new plan called for the election of Board members, without electing particular individuals to specific commissions. The Board then organized into six separate commissions of seven members each. But the major change that the new plan introduced was in the calling of deacons.

Up until then, only married couples served as deacons, but the new plan advocated calling of deacons regardless of marital status. The plan stated, "In light of our understanding of New Testament teachings on forgiveness, redemption and reconciliation (I John 1:9), the church will accept all persons, regardless of marital status, to serve as deacons." This decision opened the office of deacon to single and divorced members. And while women had served alongside their husbands as deacons previously, for the first time a woman could be called to the deacon office with or without a husband.

By 1990, the number of deacon teams had grown from 12 to 20. In a November 1990 Council Meeting report, Pastor Ross reflected on progress made: "That decision to not make marital status a condition for the calling of deacons," he wrote, "has made the Deacon Board much more accessible to our membership." As evidence he cited the growth in the number of deacons and stated a goal of reaching 25-30 deacon teams, comprised of both couples and singles.

Pastor Ross felt the changes in the deacon office, the enlargement of the Deacon Board, and renewed emphasis on their role led to a strengthened caring program of the church, as deacons now focused on spiritual matters and worked alongside salaried pastors.

As the number and role of deacons grew, pastors and deacons began to focus attention on congregational commitment. Evidence of a lack of commitment was evident on a number of fronts, including a struggle to find persons willing to serve in church offices and a wide gap between membership and attendance.

The 1986 reorganization had left the congregation with a large Church Board of more than 40 members. The guiding philosophy continued to be that a large Board afforded more opportunities for members to be involved in the life of the church. But members weren't taking advantage of those opportunities. It increasingly was becoming a burden to fill ballot positions. Unable to find 28 nominees for 14 Board positions, in April 1989 the Board presented a ballot that did not include two nominees for each ballot position. October 1989 Church Board minutes record: "Verna Moseman voiced her concern about the overall lack of commitment for our church programs. Also the lack of people willing to assume leadership roles. The Church Board agreed that this is a problem that we should all give serious and prayerful thought and consideration in trying to find a solution."

April 1991 Board minutes reported that just 22 out of 76 people who were asked to be on the ballot consented. By spring 1992, the ballot included just 18 nominees for the 14 Board positions and only one nominee for the church clerk position. In his May 1992 Council Meeting report Pastor Moyer expressed concern about the difficulty of finding people willing to be placed on the ballot for church offices. At a September 1992 Board meeting, the first four candidates asked to serve as Board chair all declined, before Henry R. Gibbel accepted.

Another sign of waning commitment was the wide gulf between church membership and attendance. While membership grew by nearly 30 percent during the Clem Rosenberger years, attendance was relatively flat. Already in the mid-1970s church attendance had fallen below half of the church membership and remained there (with the exception of 1982, when attendance averaged 390 and membership stood at 777). As part of the revitalization of the deacon body and in accordance with the new church organizational structure that was adopted in 1986, the deacons turned their attention to encouraging commitment in the congregation as a whole. The Plan of Organization stated, ". . . the congregation shall provide its members with annual opportunities to examine their faith and calling and to renew or reaffirm their relationship with the church"—a role that used to be filled by the annual deacon visit.

In March 1990, the church held the first of three annual Covenant Renewal Services. Guest preacher Curtis Dubble delivered the message and each member in attendance was invited to sign a recommitment card. After three years, the Deacon Board reviewed the membership to, in Pastor Ross' words in a newsletter column, "determine if there are persons who need to be contacted regarding their lack of attendance, involvement, and support of the church." Pastor Ross emphasized that the goal was not to drop people from the membership list, but to "make this a time of renewal as we all consider seriously what it means to be a part of the church. . . ."

Growing out of this process, beginning in 1993 the church directory categorized members as active, associate, inactive/separated, or non-resident. Of 770 total members, 611 were listed as active. Worship attendance averaged 369. After the three-year covenant renewal process, deacons continued to monitor membership on an annual basis and re-designated members when appropriate.

Women in Ministry

While wives of male deacons had served as deaconesses for many years, the 1986 organizational plan opened the deacon office to single women (or married women serving without their husbands). The following summer, the congregation would demonstrate openness to women ministers, as well. Rebecca Baile Crouse served the congregation as a summer pastoral intern from Bethany Theological Seminary from June to August 1987, the first female in a pastoral role. While the Lititz congregation in earlier days would not have accepted a female in a credentialed ministry role, and many Brethren congregations, even today, maintain scruples against female pastors, Becky, and her husband, Jerry, were well accepted that summer. "That was a good summer for all of us," recalls Jimmy. "There was no controversy."

Both Jimmy and Ralph were supportive of women in ministry, as was their predecessor Clem Rosenberger, whose sister Nancy Rosenberger Faus was an ordained Church of the Brethren minister providing leadership at the denominational seminary. After many years of open discussion in Sunday school and other settings, the Lititz Brethren were ready to embrace this change. Further evidence of that openness was demonstrated in November 1990 when the congregation voted to license Donna Walton to the ministry, and again in 1992, when the congregation licensed Wendi Hutchinson (now Wendi Hutchinson Ailor) in May and Twyla Rowe in November.

In 1994 Tracy Wenger Sadd became the first ordained woman to serve on the church staff. Since her tenure, with the exception of brief interim periods, the congregation always has had a female on the pastoral staff, some credentialed and some not, but none yet serving in a primary preaching role.

The congregation has called out three additional women to serve in ministry since the 1990s, including Nancy Fittery (licensed August 1999, ordained January 2005), Lisa Krieg (licensed June 2002, ordained January 2007), and Pamela Reist, who joined the staff as part-time Director of Christian Nurture in 2000 and was subsequently licensed (February 2002) and ordained (June 2004), after which she moved into an associate pastor role. In many of these cases, the Ministry Commission took an active role in initiating conversations and calling out gifts for ministry that they saw in members of the church.

The congregation ordained two ministers on the same day on February 22, 1998. David Longenecker, a Lititz member serving as Associate District Executive, was ordained in a morning service, and Twyla Rowe, who was serving as associate pastor in the Conestoga congregation, was ordained in the evening in a joint service with Lititz and Conestoga.

Programs and Planning

From its early days, when Lititz provided leadership for Brethren-related institutions like Elizabethtown and Juniata Colleges and The Brethren Home and Orphan's Home in Neffsville, Lititz was connected to the larger Church of the Brethren. Those ties remained strong during the late '80s and early '90s as Lititz enrolled in three denominational programs aimed at strengthening congregations. Lititz agreed to participate in the People of the Covenant small group Bible study program when it began in fall 1984, gathering regularly in "covenant groups" for prayer, study, and sharing, using Bible study curricula provided by Brethren Press. Each group met for three 10-week sessions during the year. Lititz would have at least one covenant group going for the next 15 years, when the program officially concluded in 1999. About 80 Lititz members participated in a group during the life of the program, including three who were involved all 15 years. Retired minister Harold Kenepp provided leadership for many of those years.

From 1987 to 1990 Lititz participated in the denomination's Adventure in Mission (AIM) stewardship emphasis program, which included educational and motivational components to increase outreach giving to support denominational ministries and the work of the local church. The program included a pledge process; a January 1987 *Lititz Observer* article reported that as a result of a presentation held the previous fall and a subsequent pledge process, 221 giving units committed $262,406 to the church, an 18 percent increase over 1986.

While still in the midst of AIM, the congregation voted in May 1988 to enroll in another denominational program—this time a three-year evangelism and church growth emphasis called Passing on the Promise. Retired Midway Church of the

Brethren pastor L. John Weaver and his wife, Flora, served as Congregational Advisors, while Cindy Martin and Donna Walton provided leadership as Coordinators within the congregation, working alongside the pastoral staff. Cindy and Donna received training through Evangelism Leaders Academies, led by prominent church growth leaders within and beyond the Church of the Brethren. A committee carried out a congregational self-study, and then the program included three annual congregational meetings that focused on the main emphases of the program: Reaching Out in Word and Deed, Inviting and Welcoming New People, Including and Involving New People, and Growing in Christian Discipleship. At these meetings, members generated ideas to address the themes in the curriculum. In addition, members participated in a two-day Friend-to-Friend training event to learn the rudiments of "friendship evangelism."

While Passing on the Promise didn't create dramatic numerical growth—membership did bump up slightly and average attendance rose from 344 in 1988 to 372 in 1991—it did raise awareness and resulted in some practical steps to invite and welcome people, among them an annual Invite-a-Friend Day held in conjunction with the "Sunday Funday" church picnic, production of a church brochure, increased attention to greeters, a monthly potluck meal so visitors could be invited to stay for lunch, some Sunday school class members wearing name tags, an organized lay effort to visit guests in their homes within 48 hours of their first attendance of worship, and some emphasis on reactivating inactive members. A May 1992 Property Commission report attributed the creation of handicapped-accessible bathrooms, purchase of wheelchairs, and removal of pews in the sanctuary to make room for wheelchairs as additional initiatives spurred by Passing on the Promise.

People Spots

Passing on the Promise concluded with a celebration dinner in June 1991. Not wanting to lose the momentum generated by this program, the Church Board the next February agreed to appoint a Long Range Planning Committee to take a sweeping look at the church's future and recommend goals and objectives. The proposal clarified, "The task of this Committee is not limited to any one phase of the Church activity or physical plant but is encouraged to prepare a comprehensive future plan of the total."

In February 1993 the Board approved the Long Range Planning Committee's recommendation to retain church growth consultant Jim Moss and use his People Spots Consultation Process to help guide the church's future. After several months of study, Moss led a congregational planning session in October 1993, attended by 121 people. The newsletter report of the meeting was headlined "Wow! What a Church Meeting!" Armed with Moss' insights and dreams and visions shared by members of the congregation at the meeting, the People Spots Committee, led by Larry Sauder, penned a comprehensive "Statement of Purpose and Dream" and an accompanying "Ten Year Long Range Plan," which was approved by the congregation at a Special Council Meeting in May 1994.

The statement of purpose highlighted fairly standard Mission Statement themes, such as bringing people to Christ, nurturing people in their faith, worshipping God, witnessing through Christian service, and upholding beliefs and practices of the Church of the Brethren. The dreams section of the document, which looked toward what the church would become by 2004, planted seeds for the two items that would dominate the church's life for much of the first decade of the new millennium—multiple worship services and a building project. Included among 10 dreams were offering more worship opportunities and improving facilities and using them to promote growth. Other dreams included increased staffing to spearhead new programs, strengthened youth and young adult ministry, and more.

The 10-year plan included 50 specific goals that had been suggested by members in the congregational meeting, with a handful to be implemented each year. For example, begin a young adult Sunday school class in Year One. Implement a second worship service in Year Two. In addition, specific worship and Sunday school attendance goals were attached to each year, projecting modest growth in the first few years and more ambitious increases as goals of the plan were to be implemented. All told, the plan envisioned growth in worship attendance from 382 to 563 and in Sunday school attendance from 318 to 468.

The plan was monitored carefully over the next decade. While many of the goals in the plan were accomplished, others did not come to fruition. Worship attendance remained stubbornly stuck between 350 and 400, with no discernable upward trend. The May 2001 Council Meeting approved a Board recommendation to revise the attendance marks downward "to represent more realistic goals." In a separate action, Council appointed an ad hoc committee to "address the attendance goals of the church." But at the end of the 10-year plan worship and Sunday school attendance both were down from 1994 levels. By the end of 2001 the congregation's attention and energy had shifted toward a major building project.

As the People Spots 10-year goals were winding down, the Church Board in 1990 embarked on a new visioning process with a new consultant. Brethren church growth advocate S. Joan Hershey led a Board retreat on November 12, 2000, that produced a new Mission Statement that received congregational approval the following week. Over the next few months, Sunday school classes and other small groups studied the statement and in May 2001 Council approved a Focus Statement—"Following in the Footsteps of Jesus"—and a revised version of the Mission Statement:

> *Our Mission is to be a Christ-centered fellowship, glorifying God, loving one another, and celebrating God's faithfulness and grace. We are committed to:*
> —*Make disciples*
> —*Serve compassionately*
> —*Encourage each other*
> —*Witness to our community and the world*
> —*Communicate Biblical truths and Brethren ideals in word and deed*

In November, Council approved a recommendation from the People Spots Committee to end its work and use the five statements from the new Mission Statement to set direction for the next five years. A Goals Committee was approved the following spring to formulate more specific goals based on the statement.

A Good Run

While flat attendance and struggles to fill ballot positions were discouraging, other signs pointed toward vitality and commitment during the 1980s and 1990s. Among those signs was the congregation's engagement in a variety of outreach ministries close to home and in faraway places.

In June 1983 church members and avid runners William Longenecker and Jeff Bradley organized the first annual Lititz Run for Peace, a 10-kilometer (6.2 miles) race that raised funds for a variety of peace-related projects. By 1990, the run had grown into the largest 10K race in Lancaster County, attracting more than 500 runners annually and raising money for a variety of causes.

Through the years it supported projects including the Brethren Service/Polish Agricultural Exchange; Heifer International; Brethren Volunteer Service; the World Friend-

Lititz distance runners Jeff Bradley—shown crossing the finish line at the 1985 race—and Dr. Bill Longenecker organized the first Lititz Run for Peace in 1983.

ship Center in Hiroshima, Japan; the Brethren World Peace Academy associated with On Earth Peace; Christian Peacemaker Teams' work in the Middle East; the Peace and Conflict Studies program at Juniata College; Habitat for Humanity; and more. At its peak, the event raised nearly $2,000 annually.

By the early 1990s, however, the race was beginning to lose steam. When participation dropped to 260 runners and earnings were down to $500 in 1995, planners decided the event had run its course. Race planners Brian Rice, Len Pelsinski, and Bill Longenecker reported in an April 1996 *Lititz Observer* article, "After prayerful consideration, the Run for Peace Committee has decided to discontinue the event." The article attributed the event's demise to "a decline in public interest in running, an increase in weekend sports opportunities for children, and rainy Saturdays the last few years" that had dampened participation.

While the Run for Peace had reached its finish line, it had had a good run. In its 13 years at Lititz, runners had logged more than 30,000 miles for peace and raised some $20,000 for peacemaking. And in 1999, the Peace Run was resurrected in Elizabethtown and lives today as a 5K run/walk hosted by the Elizabethtown Church of the Brethren. It continues to promote fitness and fellowship and raise funds for peace-related causes.

A Shelter in a Time of Storm

Another long-running ministry began about the same time as the Run for Peace. A speaker from the Lancaster County Council of Churches one Sunday in 1983 raised awareness of homelessness and the need for emergency housing. Rodney

AN ONGOING COMMITMENT TO PEACE

The annual Run for Peace was just one of many expressions of the congregation's ongoing commitment to peacemaking. While individual members had been free to choose military service from World War II on, the congregation continued to find ways to advocate for peace. At the conclusion of the first Iraq war (known as Operation Desert Storm), in April 1991 Pastor Ross wrote a newsletter column on "The Way of the Cross, the Way of Peace," in which he reflected on troubling aspects of the recent conflict. Among them were the "extreme display of nationalism and patriotism," a lack of concern for the suffering of Iraqi people, "the mistaken assumption that evil can be overcome by evil," and the "false contention that God takes sides in war." Pastor Ross stated strongly, "War is sin, war is failure. War is the admission that we don't believe or practice what Jesus taught."

In fall 1994 the congregation began participating in the Parenting for Peace and Justice Network to improve peacemaking at the family level. The following September the *Observer* reported that Lititz member "Jim Gibbel is being recognized for his many years of service on the On Earth Peace Assembly's Board of Directors" at an October Recognition Dinner in New Windsor, Maryland. "We commend Brother Jim for his peacemaking activities." Jim for many years also actively promoted peace through the Brethren Peace Fellowship in Atlantic Northeast and Southern Pennsylvania Districts.

But how to promote peace without causing offense to others in the church could be tricky, as shown by a 2003 attempt to tweak the church's wedding policy. The board rejected proposed language: "Military attire is not appropriate for weddings in the Church of the Brethren." Instead, the policy remained as it had been: "Military weddings are limited to the wearing of dress uniforms."

More than once the congregation sponsored the Lancaster County Peace Essay Contest. Begun in 1981 by the Lancaster Friends Meeting, the annual contest encouraged senior high youth to write essays promoting peace. When Lititz hosted the 2004 contest, the theme was "The Power of Peace in a World of Conflict." A newsletter article noted that Lititz member Julia Boyer had won in her age category the previous year.

In June 2004, the congregation installed a Peace Pole in front of the church as a visible witness to its desire for peace. The simple pole, located to the right of the church's main entrance, includes the words "May Peace Prevail on Earth" in English, Spanish, German, and French. The pole was one of some 200,000 erected in 180 countries, representing a desire for peace shared by much of the world.

Another lasting peace witness was established in 2012, when $15,000 from a $40,195 bequest from the estate of Jefferson Crosby was set aside for the Jefferson Crosby Endowment Fund for Peace and Justice. Crosby had died on January 5, 2010, after living many years with the debilitating effects of multiple sclerosis. As an attorney with Gibbel, Kraybill & Hess, he had received the Louise G. Herr Award in recognition of his work as a mediator and provider of pro bono legal services. Though he was diagnosed with MS shortly before moving into Lititz in the early 1980s, he was active in the Lititz congregation for many years, serving as moderator from 1988 to 1993.

and Verna Moseman owned a mobile home on Broad Street next to their Bicycle World business; they offered it to the Witness Commission for use as an emergency shelter. The church agreed to take on the project.

Under the umbrella of the Witness Commission, Oren Spangenburg and Ruth Husser were primary coordinators of the ministry, which provided 30 days of shelter (with some extensions) to families referred by the Council of Churches, Lutheran Social Services, and other agencies. Referring agencies sometimes provided casework services for the families, while the church focus was housing. Each month a different family from the church served as liaison, checking in with the residents at least once a week, providing occasional transportation for groceries, and cleaning the shelter when a family left. Church members also donated furnishings and assisted with maintenance. In 1988 an area dealer donated a mobile home to replace the original and the ministry continued.

The shelter was nearly always occupied for a number of years. Witness Commission chair Jeannine Boyer reported to the November 1989 Council Meeting that a total of 28 people had received shelter during the previous year, and thanked Ruth Husser for her work.

The same report highlighted other housing-related work of the congregation. The Commission had promoted two area homelessness conferences that Lititz members attended, presenting information at one on their shelter ministry. A yard sale held at the church raised $225 for the shelter ministry. And Lititz had become a Covenant Church supporting the work of Habitat for Humanity "to make the dream of decent shelter a reality for families in Lancaster and around the world." As partners with Habitat, the church provided volunteers to build houses locally, attended a fundraising banquet and local house dedications, and fed volunteers. Further from home, members Kelly Longenecker and Beth Crosby in 1989 participated in Habitat work camps in South Carolina and Nicaragua, respectively.

The report also highlighted the group of eight volunteers who had traveled to South Carolina the previous December to rebuild homes for victims of Hurricane Hugo. Volunteers were Dwight Walton, John Shenk, Kevin Shenk, Bonni Oetama, Jean de Perrot, Richard Landis, Carl Martin, and Graybill Hollinger.

By 1991, the congregation's own shelter ministry was showing some signs of strain, as the number of Lititz liaisons had dropped from 12 to 6. A January 1992 *Observer* article hinted that some of the families that had been receiving shelter had serious problems that caused some to hesitate to volunteer as liaisons. As a result more care was being given to screening clients.

By January 1994, Ruth put out an urgent newsletter plea for help, with a testimony from a former resident, and a threat that the program was in danger of closing. A month later, she lauded the congregation for "the overwhelming response." Twenty-three people came forward to serve as liaisons and the Disciples Class agreed to clean the facility between clients. With renewed interest, the shelter ministry continued for three more years, before being closed by the Witness Commission on March 7, 1997. A newsletter article attributed the closure to changing needs in the society and the social services arena. The Commission summarized, "(The shelter) helped many families during difficult times and provided many persons with the opportunity for a new beginning."

RECYCLING WHEN RECYCLING WASN'T COOL

Along with its attention to homelessness during the late '80s and early '90s, the church was growing increasingly aware of environmental issues. The two came together in a short-lived recycling effort to save the environment and also raise funds for the shelter ministry. The Witness Commission in 1989 established a Recycling Committee "to educate the congregation on ways to be better stewards of our environment." Beginning in January 1990, the church sponsored a monthly recycling Saturday for members to drop off newspapers, cans, glass, and some plastics at the church. Detailed instructions were provided on how to meticulously separate items. A newsletter article emphasized, "We recycle because we care about God's good earth."

Funds raised through the effort supported the shelter ministry, but nobody was getting rich off of the project. The first month raised $43.00, before dropping to $25.00 and $24.00 in February and March. The April 22 worship service focused on an Earth Day theme with Pastor Moyer preaching on "What on Earth Are We Doing?"

An October 1990 newsletter article announced the discontinuation of the church recycling project, noting that other options were available in the community. A November Witness Commission report explained that the project was becoming larger than planners could handle, and the borough was instituting a recycling program. While the monthly recycling at the church was short-lived, it did indicate that the Lititz Brethren were early adopters of a practice that would become widespread in coming years. To adapt an old country song, Lititz was recycling when recycling wasn't cool. And the project did raise a few dollars for the shelter ministry.

Refugees From Russia

The church provided shelter of a different kind, as it continued its longtime commitment to resettling refugees. According to a June 6, 2007, *Lancaster Online* article, from 1988 to 1992 a wave of evangelical Christian refugees from Russia were resettled in Lancaster County, with assistance from Mennonite and other churches. This was during the period of *glasnost* in the former Soviet Union, when the U.S. and Soviet governments made agreements allowing Soviet Christians to emigrate. More than 2,000 people of Russian background were living in Lancaster County by 1990, with a heavy concentration in the Ephrata area.

The Lititz Brethren in fall 1989 committed to assisting one such family through PRIME-Ecumenical Commitment to Refugees. A committee headed by Chris Oetama and Dwight Walton made arrangements for the family to live at 129 Liberty Street in a home provided by Jean de Perrot. More than 30 church members helped prepare for the family's arrival by donating furnishings, household items, and food; sprucing up the property; and more.

The Bilik family arrived on March 23, 1990, and were welcomed officially by a shower sponsored by the Lamplighter's Sunday school class. The family consisted of five members, three of whom were named Alexander! There was Alexander and his wife, Nataliya; daughter, Valentina; and son, Alexander. Also included was a brother-in-law whose first name was Alexander. The Biliks already had other family members living in the area, which eased their transition to a new land.

Fighting Hunger

Alleviating hunger is another cause that Lititz Brethren have enthusiastically supported through the years. CROP Walks to benefit the hunger relief ministries of Church World Service (CWS) are recognized by some as the first of many fundraiser walks that exist today. The first CROP Walk in the nation was held in 1969. A walk began in Lancaster in 1973, and over time churches organized additional community walks that are considered part of a countywide effort, including one in Lititz in the early 1980s. Lititz Brethren were early participants in the local CROP Walk and continue to participate today. Ralph Moyer chaired the event for the first decade or so and encouraged participation. In 1990, he reported that 22 Lititz members participated in the walk, including eight Youth Club members. Ralph sweetened the deal for youth clubbers that year by offering a sundae at Sundae Best to any youth who raised $100 or more. Angie Oetama and Ethan Gibbel were fighting for top fundraising honors, and Ralph was expecting to have to shell out for four or five sundaes, plus one for himself.

According to a 1992 newsletter article, 12 participants from Lititz raised $1,840, more than a third of the total raised by all participants in the Lititz walk. (Ralph Moyer raised $1,000 of that amount himself from 92 donors.) Among the participants were Dr. Bill Longenecker, who "walked the entire 10 kilometers pushing his twin sons, Billy and Bobby, in a wheelbarrow!" By 1994 the Lancaster County walks had raised more than $1 million for CWS.

The walk has changed locations through the years, moved from the country to town, went from 10 miles, to 10 kilometers, to shorter than that, and has seen participation decrease. But Lititz Brethren participation has been constant.

At the October 16, 2011, walk hosted by St. James Catholic Church, the 15 Brethren walkers were a full quarter of the 60 total participants. The Brethren hosted the event in 2013.

For a decade during the 1980s and 1990s the Lititz congregation hosted another event to fight hunger—an annual Living Gift Fair to support Heifer International. Sponsored by

In September 1988 the church supported another heifer-related outreach. The church's Vacation Bible School donated a steer named "Jacobson," raised by John E. Shenk, to the Brethren Disaster Relief Auction in Lebanon. Pictured with John and Jacobson are Lititz children (front from left) Jason Walton, Kelly Forney, Ashley Bomberger, Nicole Oetama, (back from left) Joel Gibbel, Joshua Walton, Todd Kurl, Jennifer Bomberger, Kirsten Crosby, Jennifer Walton, Angie Oetama, and Ethan Gibbel.

an ecumenical group of volunteers, the event provided an opportunity for alternative gift buying. The fair first was held in 1988 at Elizabethtown College, before moving to Lititz the following year. Held the Saturday of Thanksgiving weekend—a day after the "Black Friday" shopping extravaganza—the fair encouraged shoppers to buy Heifer animals and other items in honor of loved ones. Also available for purchase were food, baked goods, Heifer merchandise, and more. Live animals and entertainment attracted children.

The event continued to grow each year. The 12th and final fair in November 1999 raised $19,500. All told, in its 11 years at Lititz the event raised well over $100,000 for Heifer, before being discontinued when a new coordinator could not be found to replace the longtime leader. The Lititz Witness Commission attempted to bring together Lititz area churches to restart the fair in 2001, getting as far as setting a date, but they ran out of time and no fair was held.

OTHER OUTREACH AND SERVICE

During Jimmy Ross' pastorate, Lititz Brethren regularly participated in denominationally-sponsored work camps for youth, disaster relief trips, and more. Wendi Hutchinson served in Brethren Volunteer Service in 1994 and 1995, extending her service to become the coordinator of denominational work camps for junior and senior high youth and young adults in 1994, before becoming Assistant Coordinator of the 1996 National Youth Conference.

In May 1994, 10 Lititz members traveled to Lybrook, New Mexico, to help remodel an all-purpose building for a Brethren-affiliated Navajo congregation. Participants were

Lucy de Perrot, Jim Eby, Nancy Erwin, Larry and Nancy Fittery, Donna Heisey, Joanne Loose, Lenny Pelsinski, and Dwight and Debbie Walton.

During the summer of 1995, 14 Lititz youth and young adults and three advisors participated in Brethren work camps in Castañer, Puerto Rico; Putney, Vermont; Orlando, Florida; Northern Ireland; and Lybrook, where the Fitterys directed a denominational camp. Sixteen youth and advisors participated in similar outreaches in 1996 and again in 1997.

Closer to home, Lititz members volunteered for the Brethren Disaster Relief Auction each fall (and continue to do so), and quilters of the church regularly crafted items to be sold at the auction.

Closer to Home

During the late 1980s and 1990s the congregation increasingly viewed its building as a resource for the community. In fall 1989 the Board gave the Warwick School District permission to use the church facility to tutor pregnant teens. At least until 1991, the school used the church building for such group instruction.

In April 1991, the Board agreed to rent two of the church's kindergarten rooms to the Lititz Community Center to house their CARE program. (A May 1992 Stewardship Commission report to Council Meeting indicated that this idea grew out of Passing on the Promise.) The lease was signed August 31, 1991, and the program began in September, offering childcare for kindergarten-age children weekdays from 10 a.m. to 6:30 p.m. Rent was $295 per month, which was intended to cover costs. Lititz Rec eventually would expand the day care program, and

Youth and advisors participating in summer work camps were consecrated during the June 25, 1995, service. Pictured are (front from left) Angie Oetama, Heidi Krieg, Pat Hershey, Sonya Martin, Kendra Renn, Mandy Zeiders, Steve Keim, (back from left) Joel Gibbel, Larry and Nancy Fittery, Ethan Gibbel, Berk Gerdes, Josh Walton, and Don Rowe.

the church would build its own outreach ministry around this community program meeting in its facility.

Further evidence of the church's community involvement was the naming of Lititz member Stephen Gibble as President of the Warwick Association of Churches in 1991, which came on the heels of his service as President of Lancaster County Council of Churches.

About this time, changes were afoot in the church office. It was reported to the congregation in February 1990 that the secretary was taking word processing classes and the church had appointed a Computer Committee. But secretary Bonnie Hutchinson would step down on September 26 after seven-and-a-half years on the job, leaving it to her replacement, Kou Kha-Moua, to help guide the church office into the computer age.

Another sign of changing times, the decades-old Crusaders Sunday school class met for the last time on July 31, 1993. The class had begun meeting in January 1938, when members of the Alexander Mack class over age 35 split off to form their own class, leaving the youngsters behind in the Mack Class. The Alexander Mack class would meet a similar fate, when the Christian Education Commission would make the difficult decision to disband the class in March 2011; too few of its remaining members were able to attend due to health and age.

In September 1994, the congregation started a semi-monthly MOPS program for Mothers of Pre-Schoolers. The program provided a Christ-centered caring ministry for young moms, who met two Wednesday mornings a month for fellowship and growth. Meeting September through May, the program averaged 19 moms, along with pre-school children, the first year. By the 1997-1998 year, participation had grown to about 35 mothers and more than 50 children. MOPS ended its run at Lititz in May 2001. By then a Wednesday evening program for the entire church had been up and running for a year, which may have contributed to the end of MOPS.

Also in September 1994, the congregation began using "Jubilee: God's Good News" children's Sunday school curriculum. The new curriculum from Brethren Press was dedicated during a special service on September 18 and would serve the church until fall 2006, when the new "Gather 'Round: Hearing and Sharing God's Good News" curriculum would take its place. Another sign of its Brethren identity and strong ties to the denomination, the Lititz congregation has consistently used Brethren children's Sunday school curriculum.

A sign of the times was the passage of an Infectious Disease Policy by the November 1994 Council Meeting. The Centers for Disease Control in 1982 for the first time used the term AIDS (Acquired Immune Deficiency Syndrome) to describe a growing public health threat. In November 1992, Pastor Ross reported that the Deacon Board was studying AIDS. By 1994, the disease had become the leading cause of death for all Americans, ages 25 to 44. Fear permeated society and churches. Lititz responded with a statement of inclusion. An Infectious Disease Policy approved by Council in November 1994 began by acknowledging that "a health crisis of enormous proportions faces the church and the world" and affirming that "the church and its people are called to be a community of healing, hope, and compassion."

The heart of the document was this statement: "The Lititz Church of the Brethren welcomes any person having AIDS, or any other serious contagious illness, to worship, fellowship, and participate in church activities." It went on to spell out what steps would be taken to protect the privacy of those with an infectious disease and prevent transmission to others in the church.

Well Endowed

The Lititz congregation had a long history of receiving bequests and estate gifts from members, but during the 1990s the congregation began establishing ongoing endowment funds designated for specific purposes. One such fund was formed in memory of a too brief life. Allyson Elizabeth Wenger was born with a life-threatening heart defect on April 20, 1993, to Jim and Kathy Jo Wenger. She died June 9 before necessary heart surgery could be performed. Pastor Ross remembers dedicating Allyson.

I would always take the baby and hold it and introduce it to the congregation. And Allyson was fussy. Jim was holding her. . . . And when I took her she just calmed down. She just totally relaxed. . . . And when I put her back in Jim's arms she started fussing again. I said to them, "If you ever need a babysitter you know where to look."

They didn't need Jimmy to babysit, but a short time later he would hold the baby again. Jimmy was called into the hospital; Baby Allyson had passed away. "And I'll never forget," says Jimmy. "Kathy Jo came to me with the baby after she had died and said, 'Would you like to hold her?' And so I held her. That was just a powerful moment for me as a pastor and a friend."

Family and friends established the Allyson Wenger Family Life Enrichment Fund to enhance the family life ministries of the church, with a focus on equipping people to negotiate life's challenges and build stronger family units.

Similarly, the Donald L. Tennis Capital Improvements Fund grew out of tragedy. The fund was established from memorial gifts after Don was killed in an auto accident by a drunk driver in 1993.

Previously, in fall 1983, the church had established the Educational Enrichment Fund, using funds from the estate of Florence B. Gibbel (1878-1971). Florence was a charter member, wife of the early minister Henry R. Gibbel, and matriarch of the congregation's Gibbel clan. She outlived her husband by more than 40 years and remained a devoted and faithful servant of Christ and the church throughout her life. In recognition of Florence's interest in teaching and learning, the fund established in her honor primarily provides scholarships to Lititz members attending seminaries and colleges, with preference given to Brethren institutions and students preparing for ministry or other areas of Christian service. In addition, the Jeremiah S. and Esther G. Longenecker Fund for Training Ministers was established from an estate gift in 1975. In 1994, the congregation voted to utilize the asset management services of Brethren Foundation, Inc., to manage these and other long-term investment funds.

Music Notes

Music and worship continued to evolve during the Ross years, as Joan Fyock served as Director of Music Ministries. In March 1988, Joan introduced a new sound to the congregation. Using bells begged from Linden Hall and music stands borrowed from Lititz United Methodist Church, Joan found eight women able to steal some time from their busy schedules to form a bell choir. Inaugural ringers Becky Brubaker, Mary Lou Hickle, Elaine Gibbel, Bonnie Hutchinson, Carol Kurl, Jeannine Boyer, Janice Wenger, and Beth Crosby practiced for six weeks before their first performance. Reviews were positive. The writer of an *Observer* article reported, "A lot of congregational enthusiasm was expressed following the service."

The following month the Worship and Fellowship Committee brought a request to the Board to purchase bells and accessories, which was approved, "providing the necessary funds are donated for this purpose prior to purchasing bells." Evidently the money came in quickly. By July, three octaves of bells and hand chimes for a youth choir were in hand. Both groups performed for the first time during a December 4 dedication service for the new bells.

The congregation's music leaders had clear musical preferences and sought to promote proper decorum in worship, as indicated by revisions to the church wedding policy approved by the Board in April 1993. "Assuming that organ music is desired," the paper began, "the church organist will assist the couple in selecting appropriate sacred and classical music for the ceremony." It went on to say, "Instrumental music should avoid association with a secular context (movie themes, recent popular recordings, etc.)."

In 1994 the congregation upgraded its instruments with the addition of a used Baldwin grand piano—a significant step up from the upright that had been used previously. Purchased with designated contributions, the instrument was dedicated during the Sunday morning worship service on February 27, followed by a celebratory evening concert featuring several church members performing sacred and classical selections.

By then congregational music leaders had a lot of new material from the new blue hymnal to work with. In 1992 the Church of the Brethren, working in cooperation with Mennonite bodies, produced its first new hymnal since the 1951 "red hymnal." Lititz was well apprised of the progress of *Hymnal: A Worship Book*, as two of its staff were intimately involved in its creation.

As the publication date approached, the Music and Worship Commission prepared by organizing a fundraiser that allowed members to donate toward the purchase of hymnals. With Carol Kurl spearheading the effort, 327 hymnals had been donated by May 1992. The new books arrived in the summer and were used in worship for the first time on July 19, followed by a dedication service on September 20. *Hymnal: A Worship Book* remains in use today at Lititz. Matching New Revised Standard Version pew Bibles were added in 1999.

In 1990 a new tradition was added to the Christmas season. To kick off Advent, the congregation held its first Old

THE MAKING OF A HYMNAL

When the Lititz congregation used its new blue hymnals in worship for the first time in July 1992, it wasn't new to everyone in the congregation. Pastor Jimmy Ross and Director of Music Ministries Joan Fyock were intimately familiar with its contents. Both had been working to shape *Hymnal: A Worship Book* for nearly eight years—and Joan wasn't finished quite yet.

Beginning in 1984, Jimmy served on the Hymnal Council. Comprised of members of the Church of the Brethren, Mennonite Church, and General Conference Mennonite Church, the Council compiled, culled through, debated (even argued over), and ultimately selected the hymns and worship resources that made the final work. Pastor Ross also served on the Worship Committee for the hymnal, the group that selected and shaped the readings, prayers, and other resources in the back of the book.

Joan was a member of the Music Committee, helping to locate, evaluate, and select hymns for inclusion in the hymnal. She and the Lititz congregation also played a major role in the production of a hymnal-related resource. Joan served as editor of *The Hymnal Companion*, a 752-page reference work that provides background and stories about many of the hymns in the blue hymnal.

In July 1988 Joan established an office to coordinate work on *The Hymnal Companion* in part of the sewing room at Lititz. Over the next four years, dozens of Lititz members helped in a variety of ways. In a November 1992 *Observer* article, Joan thanked Lititz members for their roles, including the quilters for sharing their room; Jeff and Brett Tennis and Ernie Forney for providing computers; Walt Keeney who gave 14 months of Tuesdays, entering data,

> filing, and assisting with writing; proofreaders Erma Forry, Lisa Krieg, Elaine Gibbel, and Janet Savage; and dozens of others who helped with clerical tasks.
>
> The article reported that the last of hundreds of articles had been sent to Brethren Press in October. *The Companion* finally was published by Brethren Press in 1996, following four more years of editing and pre-publication work by Lani Wright.

Tyme Christmas Gathering on Sunday, December 2. The 5:30 p.m. event featured a full turkey dinner, with members providing the trimmings, followed by carol singing, and some special music. For a number of years a skit by Jimmy and Betty Ross and Ralph and Annette Moyer was a much anticipated feature of the lighthearted gathering. "As I recall," says Jimmy, "I think a number of those shocked some people. I think we did some things that weren't quite as dignified as some people thought it should be."

While the menu and program varied from year to year, the basic recipe of an evening meal, seasonal music, and some mirth to begin the Advent season remained unchanged until the Old Tyme Gathering came to an end in 1998. It was replaced in 1999 by an Advent Festival, where members were encouraged to come to the church for some caroling, followed by decorating of Sunday school rooms and eating sundaes.

A lasting change to the congregation's Christmas celebration came in December 1993, when a second Christmas Eve Service was introduced. Since then the congregation has hosted a family-oriented service early in the evening and a more reverent late service each year.

Adding a Second Service

While the church had added a second Christmas Eve service in 1993, Sunday mornings continued to feature a traditional church schedule of Sunday school at 9 a.m., followed by a single worship service at 10:30. But a number of area churches had begun to offer multiple services to cater to preferences in worship times or styles, involve more people in leading worship, or to make room for more worshippers. Lititz had stated its intention to launch a second service in May 1994, when it approved a 10-year plan that called for a second service "early in year two." With worship attendance averaging 385 during 1994, sanctuary seating was snug. And church growth experts familiar to the congregation through Passing on the Promise had warned of a psychological barrier that prevented attendance from growing beyond 80 percent of a sanctuary's seating capacity. To make room for more worshippers and involve more people in leading worship, Lititz looked toward a second service.

The Worship and Fellowship Commission appointed a committee of six to plan for the new service. Referring to themselves as the "3S Committee" (Second Sunday Service), members Pam Eckert, Polly Gibble, Lenny Pelsinski, Janet Savage, Ernest Shenk, and Garth Becker had conversations with eight other churches who had moved to a multiple service format, before recommending that an 8 a.m. service be added to the church schedule. The times of Sunday school and the main service remained unchanged.

While the early service would feature the same sermon as the main service, it would utilize lay worship leaders and rely on musicians other than the church staff to lead music and provide special music. This proposal was approved for a six-month trial period, and the new service met for the first time on April

23, 1995, in the church sanctuary. It continued after the trial period. A year later it was reported that the service was going well, and a 1997 newsletter article reported that the previous year 29 different people had served as soloists during the early service.

Because the sanctuary was getting full and the new service steered clear of worship style debates, the 8 a.m. service was noncontroversial, members say. But some had hoped the second service would be more contemporary than it ended up being. "We wanted it to be a different style," one member recalls, "but with the people that came at 8 a.m. it ended up being pretty much a traditional style worship service. But it was like, 'What happened here?' We wanted it to be a different style and we ended up having the same style."

The 8 a.m. service developed a loyal following, appealing to people seeking a less formal service and early-rising older members of the congregation. Those desiring a different worship style would have to wait for nearly a decade, and the second time around adding a new service would be a lot more complicated than the first.

A Deteriorating Building

By the time the congregation finished celebrating its 75th anniversary in 1989, the state-of-the-art building that had been dedicated in 1962 and expanded in 1969 was showing some signs of age. The nearly 30-year-old roof needed work and, on the ground, the parking lot required resurfacing. But money was tight.

One option for raising cash was selling a former parsonage on Second Avenue, across from the church, but the Board rejected a Property Commission proposal to do so in February 1989. The matter was discussed again in fall 1991. After doing a thorough cost/benefit analysis, the Stewardship Commission recommended keeping the property. In the meantime, the condition of the church roof and the parking lot weren't improving. So in April 1991 the congregation had taken out a $95,000 line of credit and got to work. The parking lot was repaved over the summer, and on November 13 the roof project was completed for some $44,000.

A third component of the facilities improvements was the installation of handicap-accessible restrooms in February 1992, a need that had been identified through Passing on the Promise. Total cost for the improvements was $94,200, according to a February 1992 newsletter report from the Stewardship Commission. To help pay down what was then considered a significant debt, the Stewards staged a "Challenge Sunday" offering on September 15, 1991, that brought in nearly $37,000. By early 1992 more than $50,000 had been given to retire the debt.

But by November Council, the financial situation had deteriorated. The Stewards reported that through the first three quarters of the year, giving was $41,544 short of budget and, as a result, benevolences to district and denominational ministries had not been paid—the first time in at least 13 years that these donations had not been made on time. At the same meeting, the Property Commission reported that the church's 30-year-old heating system was on its last leg and recommended major upgrades at a cost of $69,000, with an additional $10,000 to install storm windows over the sanctuary windows. The commission recommended borrowing the money to do the project immediately, before the church got left in the cold. The report noted that expected savings on gas of $600 per month as a result of the upgrade would cover the monthly loan payments.

The congregation continued to observe annual Challenge Sundays to pay down the debt, which finally was retired in November 1994, thanks in part to a matching contribution of $14,735 from the Don Tennis Memorial Fund. While building improvements costing less than $200,000 in the early 1990s posed a challenge for the congregation, a major project a decade later would be measured in millions, not thousands, and would pose a far greater challenge.

Changing of the Guard

One disadvantage of having two pastors of similar age and experience is that they reach the same life and career stages together. In the case of Pastors Ross and Moyer, both came due for a sabbatical and looked toward retirement at about the same time. Jimmy Ross took the first part of a sabbatical March 23-June 3, 1990, when he served as Pastor in Residence at Bethany Theological Seminary. (In 1992, he also would serve on the Search Committee that called Eugene Roop as the seminary president.) In summer 1992, Jimmy and Betty participated in a three-week European Brethren Heritage Tour led by Donald and Hedda Durnbaugh. Ralph helped cover for Jimmy during his two sabbatical stints.

Jimmy had the opportunity to return the favor in 1994, when Ralph scheduled his first sabbatical in 30 years in two five-week segments. First, in January/February he participated in a Nigeria work camp, and then in July/August Ralph and Annette would travel in Europe, including two weeks of study in Budapest, Hungary, and time in Austria, Switzerland, and Germany. The Ministry Commission invited the congregation to show appreciation for Ralph's 14 years of ministry among them by contributing love gifts to help cover Annette's travel and Ralph's incidental expenses.

Even as the Ministry Commission and pastors were planning and participating in sabbaticals, they also were looking down the road to when Jimmy and Ralph would retire. Already in November 1993—more than four years before either would retire—the commission appointed a Pastoral Consultation Committee to help prepare and plan for the day when their longtime ministry team would move on. As part of the preparation, for a time both pastors and their wives participated in a weekly seminar at Elizabethtown College. And they discussed ways of easing the transition for the congregation.

But Jimmy and Ralph weren't coasting toward retirement. Both remained active in the congregation and beyond. Ralph was a mainstay on the Board of Camp Swatara, and Jimmy during the mid-1990s served on the District Goals for the '90s Committee and on the Annual Conference Standing Committee. Then the 1996 Annual Conference called Jimmy to serve as the moderator of the 1998 Annual Conference, the highest elected office in the Church of the Brethren. Speaking of his denominational involvements, Jimmy explains, "I did those things with the encouragement of the congregation. The Ministry Commission felt—and I think the congregation felt—that Lititz had a responsibility to provide leadership for the larger church. I didn't allow my name to go on the ballot for Annual Conference moderator because I wanted to be moderator. But they encouraged me to be moderator because they felt I could do it and that Lititz could afford to do it."

As things turned out, he would not fulfill his term as moderator. While serving as moderator-elect, Jimmy was diagnosed with prostate cancer and had surgery on May 28, 1997, followed by several weeks of recovery. When a period of depression followed his brush with cancer, he asked to be relieved of his moderator responsibilities. Former moderator Elaine Sollenberger took his place. Back at Lititz, during his medical absence Pastor for Nurture Tracy Sadd, former Pastor for Nurture Henry Renn, and Bob Kettering helped Ralph Moyer cover Jimmy's pastoral responsibilities.

But Ralph also was preparing for his own retirement. Early in 1997, he informed the congregation that he would conclude his ministry at Lititz. In an April newsletter column he reflected on Ecclesiastes 3:1: "There's a time for beginnings and a time for endings; a time for starting a ministry, and a time for retiring and leaving." His time of beginning had been July 1, 1980; his chapter at Lititz would close on December 31. On January 4, 1998, the congregation held an appreciation service for Ralph. Jimmy Ross and Robert Kettering led worship, and longtime pastor and friend Curtis Dubble preached.

Things turned a bit more light-hearted after the service as the congregation gathered for a meal, with emcee Larry Sauder presiding over a roast of their beloved pastor. The program included appearances by surprise guests and presentation of gifts, including a quilt made by the ladies of the church, $1,500 in cash, custom pottery made by member Steve de Perrot, and a scrapbook of memories of Ralph's more than 17 years of ministry at Lititz.

While the morning service and dinner were an appropriate commemoration of Ralph's faithful service, his departure from the congregation was short-lived. After a part-time interim pastorate at Hempfield Church of the Brethren, Ralph returned in 1999 for a stint as interim Pastor for Christian Nurture, and since November 2007 has served the congregation as part-time volunteer Pastor of Visitation.

Robert D. Kettering, who already had been a member of the congregation for several years and served on district and then denominational staff, began as interim Pastor for Special Ministries on January 1, 1998, joining Pastors Ross and Sadd.

With Ralph's service concluded and appropriately celebrated, Jimmy implemented the next step of the plan by announcing his retirement, effective September 1, 1998. A special service on September 20 celebrated Jimmy's 15 years of service. Ralph Moyer preached for his longtime colleague and friend. Again, the congregation hosted a dinner following the service as a sendoff for Jimmy and Betty, which featured sharing of memories and presentations of gifts. Reflecting on the day in a subsequent newsletter article, Jimmy observed, "The outpouring of recognition and appreciation was overwhelming. We're still trying to deal with the reality that we were so richly blessed and so strongly affirmed. We wonder if we deserve all that was said, given, and done. But we are confident that all this, along with 'every good gift,' comes from the touch of God's grace."

The following spring Pastor for Christian Nurture Tracy Sadd would conclude her service with the congregation, the final member of the "Dream Team" that had schooled others at Annual Conference on the rudiments of successful team ministry. Within 15 months, the congregation's three primary leaders would leave. But it was a good run for Ralph and Jimmy and the other pastors who joined the team for a time. Jimmy remembers it as a shared ministry and a meaningful ministry, made more so by the continuity that the pastors and congregation enjoyed.

"We were able to experience much of what free ministry churches experience," he observes, "with pastors who stay there and who are part of that congregation."

Ralph affirms the importance of longevity. "Working in a congregation this long has its rewards," he says, "because you dedicate little babies, and then you baptize them as teenagers, and then even stay long enough to do their wedding ceremonies."

CHAPTER 6

Ministry in the New Millennium

ASSEMBLING A NEW TEAM

Bob Kettering was the first piece of a new pastoral team. Upon Jimmy's retirement, Bob went from being Ralph's temporary replacement to Jimmy's, assuming responsibilities as interim pastor on September 1. Dana Statler joined the team as interim associate pastor at that time and served for one year. From there, things moved quickly. At a Special Council Meeting on October 21, 1998, the congregation voted to remove the "interim" from Bob's title and call him as pastor. He was officially installed on January 24, 1999. Easing the transition was the fact that Bob and his family had been members at Lititz for some 11 years prior to his call.

At a June 8, 1999, Special Council Meeting, the congregation called Stephen R. Hess to serve as associate pastor. Steve, Betty, and sons David and Michael, moved to Lititz in August, and Steve began work on September 7. He came to Lititz from the Pottstown Church of the Brethren, where he had been solo pastor for 14 years. The newsletter article introducing him observed that Steve's skills were a good match for a position description that focused on visitation, small groups, and family life. Steve and Bob would form the core of another long-serving pastoral team. (They continue in their roles at this writing.)

Jan Havemann, a member of the congregation and daughter of former Pastor Clem Rosenberger, was named interim Director of Youth Ministries in November 1999 and installed as Director in January 2000. Finally, Director of Christian Nurture Pam Reist came on board May 1, 2000. (Neither Jan nor Pam came with ministerial credentials, but the congregation would license Pam in 2002, at which point she became Pastor of Christian Nurture. After completing her seminary education, she was ordained in 2004 and continued to provide a fruitful ministry at Lititz for several more years.) Making it nearly a clean sweep, even longtime custodian Paul Groff retired August 31, 2000, and was replaced by Don Rowe. Don joined Carl Martin, who had begun work in the newly created Maintenance Manager position on January 1.

Licensed minister Jeff Glisson, who moved into the congregation in 1999 and was subsequently relicensed at Lititz, served as pastoral intern from October 2000 to April 2001. Jeff eventually would choose not to pursue ordination, but has actively served the congregation in a variety of lay leadership roles.

The wholesale changing of the guard in the church office created opportunities to evaluate existing ministries and impetus to make not all things, but some things, new. One of the first changes was the implementation of a new plan of organization. Prior to Bob becoming pastor, the Board had been studying the plan of organization. For many years, the church had been groaning under the weight of a large Board. It had grown increasingly difficult to find candidates willing to be placed on the ballot. At a Special Council Meeting in March 1998 the congregation approved a revised plan. Commissions were reduced from seven members each to five, and the size of the Board shrank from 43 to 31. More significant was the move from a ballot to a slate. Instead of *electing* Board members from nominees provided by the Personnel and Nominating Committee, now the church would *call* leaders from a slate presented by a Gifts Discernment Team. In a newsletter column, Pastor Kettering explained the change as a move away from "winners and losers" in elections to a process of discerning and affirming spiritual gifts of those called to serve. On a practical level, the smaller Board and the need to present only one candidate per position reduced the burden on those seeking people to serve. At the same time, the new system of calling gave the congregation less "say" in who would serve. While the congregation still had the final word, the Gifts Discernment Team became the body that for all practical purposes determined the church's leadership.

The Board continued to tinker with organizational structure, and in November 2003 the congregation approved more changes, the most significant of which was what one member described as a further "slimming down of the Board." Instead of all commission members serving on the Board, now only the chair and vice-chair of each commission, plus various *ex officio* members, would attend Board meetings, cutting the size of the Board by half. In addition, the Executive Committee would meet only in case of emergency between Board meetings to eliminate having to transact business twice at the Executive Committee and Board levels. Finally, the number of commissions increased from six to seven when the Worship and Fellowship Commission was divided to form two new Commissions: Music and Worship and Fellowship and Hospitality.

Wednesday Nights ALIVE

As a new millennium dawned, the long-running Youth Club program gave way to new mid-week programming for all ages. Begun in 1967, Youth Club was an after school program for older elementary and middle school-age youth. But by the late 1990s the program was losing steam.

"Things changed in the school system," observed Pastor Kettering. "Wednesdays used to be a day when the school system said there are no school activities. Wednesday was a great time. Kids could come right over from school here." Faced with waning attendance and growing competition from the schools, early in 2000 the church appointed a committee to evaluate Youth Club. They recommended that it be replaced with a midweek program for all ages.

What became known as Wednesday Nights ALIVE (Abundant Living in Varied Experiences) kicked off on September 27, 2000. Patterned after similar programs in other churches, Wednesday Nights ALIVE began with a meal and then consolidated a variety of church activities on Wednesday night. It offered two one-hour slots for education, choir rehearsals, committee meetings, and more. Initially it included an informal monthly worship service, something that had been called for in the People Spots goals. Performing at the inaugural session of Wednesday Nights ALIVE was well-known Brethren ventriloquist Steve Engle, and the first educational sessions were a COBYS Family Services parenting program and an Alpha curriculum study of "What Christianity Is All About."

Though some of the times and details changed through the years, and the program has had its ups and downs, the basic formula for a church night at midweek has endured. Wednesday Nights ALIVE continues.

AN UNWELCOME VISITOR

Generally, the Lititz congregation is glad to welcome guests, but one Friday in May 1999 an unwelcome visitor dropped in unexpectedly. A frightened whitetail deer wandered into the cul-de-sac formed by the chapel, print shop, and kitchen area. When she got spooked, rather than exiting to the open side toward Second Avenue, she crashed through a window into the old church print shop and bolted into the fellowship hall. Seeing the light, the disoriented deer smashed through the next window into the courtyard. After frantically searching for an escape route, she vaulted onto the tunnel roof adjacent to the sanctuary and hurtled herself against the sanctuary window, leaving evidence of her struggle some eight feet high on the window. She finally broke through and tumbled into the sanctuary, where the badly injured animal eventually collapsed.

Joan Fyock Norris provided some written notes on the event some years later from the perspective of a music staff person. She observed that the deer shed blood around the organ console and eventually was euthanized by a State Game Commission officer "in the second row of the choir area (soprano section)."

At a couple points the deer had squeezed through a single pane, leaving the window sashes intact. But she left behind a trail of broken glass, stains on windows and doors, and a bloody mess in the sanctuary, all of which needed to be cleaned up before Sunday.

A New Year's Tradition

On January 1, 2000, the Lititz Brethren began a new tradition—or at least put their mark on the very old tradition of getting the New Year off to a good start by eating pork and sauerkraut. The annual New Year's Day dinner at the church began as a joint effort of the Seekers Sunday school class and the senior high youth. The goal was to create the Lititz Church of the Brethren Youth Foundation—an investment fund whose interest would be used to fund youth programming and relieve youth and advisors from incessant fundraising to pay the way to National Youth Conference, work camps, and other events.

With a plan in place, Rodney Young took a truck to the Brethren Disaster Relief Auction in September 1999 and filled it with 165 large heads of cabbage. The following day 13 youth and 19 adults sliced and pickled the cabbage into freshly made sauerkraut. In mid-October, 12 members of the Seekers' class prepared 110 quarts of applesauce in two-and-one-half hours. After much more planning and publicizing, the New Year arrived, and the first annual dinner was a huge success. The church served 850 people in four hours, and earned more than $7,000! A newsletter report credited Rodney Young: "It was his vision and leadership that inspired and energized this effort. He put much of himself into making it a success."

By 2002, the Youth Foundation Fund had grown to more than $24,000 and the annual New Year's Dinner had become a fixture. In 2003 more than 100 volunteers, led by Rodney and Carol Young, Carol Kurl, and Marty Hershey, served 893 meals and raised $7,100. Along with consuming 600 pounds of roast pork, 350 pounds of potatoes, and 60 gallons of kraut, those attending were treated to musical entertainment by members of the church. In 2005 planners took the event to the next level, seeking business support to help provide meals to shut-ins and persons unable to afford their own "good luck" dinner. The New Year's event now was good fortune not only for the people who enjoyed the meal and music, and for the youth who benefitted from the

Rodney Young, shown here serving up pork and kraut in 2013, has been a moving force behind the annual New Year's Dinner. (Above) The pork is roasted in a portable cooker, manned here by Ken Hess.

funds raised, but also those who could enjoy a meal provided through the generosity of others.

In 2014, the New Year's tradition continued to be good luck for all concerned, as 175 volunteers worked over two days to prepare food and serve more than 1,000 people at the church and another 800 who received take-outs. Profit generated was $16,500, which would help Lititz youth attend National Youth Conference in Colorado later in the year. All told, in its first 15 years, the dinner raised more than $200,000 for the Youth Foundation Fund.

A Nuevo Relationship

In fall 2000 the Lititz Brethren became aware of a mission partnership opportunity with a fledgling Church of the Brethren fellowship in Bethlehem, Pa. At about the same time the congregation received a $210,000 bequest from the estate of longtime members Paul and Estella Irvin, 90 percent of which was designated for outreach.

Nuevo Amanecer (New Dawn) Fellowship was renting space in a Lutheran church that was not centrally located in the largely Spanish-speaking neighborhood that they hoped to serve. The Bethlehem Brethren had opportunity to purchase an ideally located church property at 501 William Street for $110,000, and believed they could handle a $25,000 mortgage. The Harrisburg First Church of the Brethren, which was in relationship with the fellowship in Bethlehem, was able to contribute $10,000 toward the purchase, leaving a $75,000 gap. After several Lititz members visited in Bethlehem and some Nuevo Amanacer members visited Lititz, in November 2000 Lititz voted 64-1 to enter into a mission partnership, using a portion of the Irvin Estate gift and inviting members to make additional contributions. In February 2001, an agreement approved by the Board hammered out the details: Lititz gave a grant of $25,000, along with individual contributions of $16,000 toward the purchase of the building, and then guaranteed a mortgage of $59,000, with Lititz Mutual Insurance Company serving as the mortgage holder. In addition, Lititz committed to pay 75 percent of each mortgage payment.

The new relationships that were formed were perhaps as important as the financial commitment. Pastor Steve Hess became a mentor and friend to the Bethlehem Brethren, and a number of Lititz members participated in the new partnership. The new building was purchased in January 2001, and in March the Lititz praise band and a busload of supporters participated in a service of celebration in the newly purchased church.

The Lititz congregation partnered with the Nuevo Amanacer congregation in Bethlehem to help them purchase a building. Lititz volunteers constructed the ramp at the building's main entrance.

During 2002 volunteers from Lititz helped build a new entrance ramp, steps, and a narthex, to go with earlier entrance work completed by Rodney Young and some of his Lebanon Building Systems employees. Another project was repointing the interior brick walls of the steeple tower. In January 2003 Lititz Brethren held a final work day at Nuevo Amanacer and delivered a used 15-passenger van that had been donated by Middle Creek Church of the Brethren to assist the church in Bethlehem. Steve reported to the May 2003 Council that the partnership with Nuevo Amanacer had marked its third anniversary. Early in 2003, it was reported that the fellowship recently had conducted 12 baptisms.

In 2013, Nuevo Amanacer and Pastor Fausto Carrasco, along with the Atlantic Northeast District, would be instrumental in petitioning Annual Conference to recognize the emerging Church of the Brethren in Spain. Had Lititz not helped the church in Bethlehem to succeed, perhaps the new Church of the Brethren in Spain would not exist or be recognized.

Focus on Families

Pam Reist's presence on staff as Director of Christian Nurture contributed to a renewed focus on children and families during the early 2000s. "One of the first things I was tasked to do," Pam recalls, "was to develop the child protection policy—or at least to take what already had been worked on and carry it a little further." Pam was well-positioned to help with this task in that she was serving on a committee of the Atlantic Northeast District to develop guidelines for congregations to create such policies. After more than a year of work and education for the church, the congregation approved its first Child Protection

Policy in November 2002. The statement provided definitions of physical, sexual, and emotional abuse and detailed steps that the church would take to protect children in its care—including the annual signing of a Children's Ministry Covenant and participation in mandatory training by those working with children and youth. Only those who had attended the congregation for at least six months and were willing to submit to a screening process would be able to work with children. A decade later the congregation would engage in an even more rigorous process to ensure the safety of children in cooperation with the Samaritan Counseling Center. Director of Christian Nurture Debbie Evans would champion this effort.

In fall 2002 a new children's ministry was launched and met with immediate success. Modeled after similar programs at Manor and Lancaster Brethren in Christ Churches, Toddler Gym would be a weekly time of activities for parents and toddlers to play together, along with a brief devotional time each week. Utilizing a $3,000 bequest from the Levi Weaver estate and some unexpended funds from the discontinued MOPS program, the congregation purchased some high quality equipment, including a maple nursery gym made by Community Playthings, a business of the Anabaptist Bruderhof Community in Rifton, New York. "We bought some really fine equipment," says Pam, "which I think made it very special for the children and their parents. We were very fortunate to have a gift from the estate of Levi Weaver, who loved children, so it seemed quite appropriate."

The committee of Ellen Harpel, Stacy McSparren, Mary Ressler, Deb Tobias, Susan Weit, and Pam planned for the grand opening on Thursday morning, October 3, 2002, and waited to see if anyone would come. "And the first time we opened the doors," Pam recalls, "we realized very quickly that we needed to have several sessions because there was just an overwhelming response. It was much greater than we ever could have imagined." A total of 37 parents and 55 toddlers showed up for the first session. Bob Kettering reported to the Council Meeting in November that the program in its first six weeks had "ministered to over 200 parents and children, many of whom have no church home." A second session was added immediately and the following fall, with the church in the midst of a building project that necessitated a move of the program to the small fellowship hall, Pam and company ran three smaller sessions.

"And we would always end each session with a little circle time with some singing and a little prayer," says Pam. "And there were people for whom that was church. Their children would sing the songs at home, and they connected with other families when they came. And when we ended our season in the springtime, when the weather was nice, some of the families had connected in such ways that they met in the park over the summer and continued their friendship."

A month after the launch of Toddler Gym, the congregation kicked off a second outreach to young children. Since 1991, the Lititz congregation had hosted a day care program run by the Lititz Rec Center. While the day care utilized the church's facilities and enjoyed positive working relationships with the congregation, there was little interaction between the church and the children. In November 2002 that changed with the beginning of Faith & Friendship Club. With parental permission, Pam Reist began meeting one morning per week with pre-school students—many of whom were not involved in a church family—for a time of singing and Bible stories. "We felt like that was a really meaningful program," Pam recalls, "for the children and for us."

Both Toddler Gym and Faith & Friendship Club continued on after Pastor Pam's departure in 2008 and have remained important outreaches. Toddler Gym currently meets Thursday and Friday mornings and Faith & Friendship follows on Fridays for seven months each year.

Reaching Out and Bringing In

Along with these new outreach ministries to children within the walls of the church, the congregation in fall 2002 began a worldwide outreach through a newfangled thing (for the Lititz Brethren, at least) called a website. The December 2002 *Observer* included an article with the bold headline: "Lititz Church Communicates Around the World." It reported that Rodney Young and Oren Spangenburg had successfully established www.lititzcob.com, the first web presence for the congregation. Five years later, in December 2007, the Board approved a new committee to redesign the site and take it to the next level, with Jonathan Charles to serve as the lead developer. Finally, in spring 2011, Pastor Steve Hess reported that a new website was up and running, and the church also recently had begun utilizing e-mail for its prayer chain.

About the same time as it first embraced the web, Jeff Glisson reported to the May 2002 Council Meeting that the church had participated in a more traditional outreach—placing Bibles that contained nameplates with some information about the church in rooms at the Warwick Inn & Suites. The hotel was owned by Lititz members Dave and Cathy Bomberger, who Jeff thanked in his report.

To help disciple new people coming into the church, in fall 2002 the congregation held its first Alpha course, with Earl Ziegler teaching 24 participants. The following spring Steve Hess led a second class of 22 in the non-denominational curriculum that grew out of a charismatic congregation in London in the late 1970s and went on to become a worldwide phenomenon. Bob Kettering reported to the November 2002 Council Meeting: "At last we have a discipleship process through the Alpha program which provides nonbelievers with a way to understand the Christian faith at a basic level and claim Christ as their Savior."

The church used Alpha for the next four years as a supplement to its regular instruction for new members and in other settings. "It was a significant experience," says Pastor Steve Hess, noting that it required a 13-week commitment from participants.

In 2005 another popular spiritual growth emphasis energized the church for a time. According to Steve Hess, some 300 people participated in 30 different groups through the 40 Days of Purpose program. Built around Saddleback Church Pastor Rick Warren's best-selling book *The Purpose Driven Life,* the spiritual growth campaign had the goal of helping people discover God's purpose for their lives. According to saddlebackresources.com, Lititz was one of more than 20,000 churches to have participated in the process.

Lay members of the congregation note that 40 Days provided opportunities for new group leaders to be challenged and develop their gifts and introduced some people to the benefits of small groups for the first time. Joel Gibbel recalls that the process led to lasting spiritual and numerical growth in the church's young adult group. "It helped the congregation to experience a diversified small group life," observes Steve Hess, noting that it took nearly a year to prepare for the 40-day experience, and that a couple groups that began then continued on a decade later.

Another opportunity for fellowship and growth got underway on October 4, 2003, when a group of men gathered at Fiorentino's Restaurant for the first monthly Men's Fellowship

Breakfast. Lititz area attorney and Middle Creek Church of the Brethren free minister Brian Black was the speaker. Ever since, the event has followed a simple formula. Gather at 7 a.m. at an area restaurant, place food orders, listen to a speaker tell his or her life story for 25 minutes, eat, and then listen to the speaker reflect on life lessons learned. Wrap up by 8:30 prompt. While the restaurant has changed from time to time, the basic format of the morning has stood the test of time. About 18 men have been gathering one Saturday each month from October through May for more than a decade to hear speakers both from within and outside of the congregation. Larry Sauder wrapped up the 11th year as speaker in May 2014. "The personal sharing about life and faith are what makes this group so special," says Steve Hess, who has been the breakfast's primary planner.

While a number of new things were getting underway in 2002, one longtime institution came to an end. In his Stewardship Commission report to the May 2003 Council Meeting, Henry R. Gibbel reported: "2002 saw the end of an era as Dr. Franklin Cassel relinquished his position as the head of our offering records team. We thank and pay special recognition to Doc Cassel for his long tenure and stewardship of his time organizing the records team, maintaining numerous reports and overseeing with diligence, the accuracy of the recording of our monetary gifts to the church."

MORE THAN A STATISTICIAN

Dr. Franklin K. Cassel was much more than a good offering counter and statistician. For decades he was a leader in the church, community, and world. As a family physician and geriatric specialist, he practiced medicine in Lititz from 1946 to 1980, when he retired and moved to Brethren Village. From 1975 to 1984 he was Medical Director at Brethren Village and served for a time in the same role at other area retirement communities.

Earlier in life, from 1944 to 1946 he served at the Church of the Brethren hospital in Castaner, Puerto Rico, and from 1950 to 1951 he was Medical Director for the United Nations Civil Assistance Command in Korea. He received citations from the commanding general of the Eighth Army in Korea and from the Ministry of Public Health in the Republic of Korea for his contributions to the field of public health there. In 1997 he received the Peacemaker of the Year Award from the Brethren Peace Fellowship.

Dr. Franklin K. Cassel

In the local church, his service included time as board chair, chair of the Building Committee that oversaw the construction of the church on Orange Street in the early 1960s, and more. "He was a constant advocate for outreach in our church budget," recalls Jim Gibbel. "At many of our Council Meetings we were reminded by Dr. Cassel of our opportunity and calling as faithful, generous supporters of the larger church and outreach organizations."

Spurred by his experiences caring for his wife, Peggy, who suffered from Alzheimer's Disease, Dr. Cassel became an activist, who sought to increase public awareness of the disease. He shared his own experiences with Alzheimer's by writing *Flowers for Peggy* in 1994. Dr. Cassel died on August 11, 2004, at age 90.

CHAPTER 7

Daunting Challenges

While the influx of new pastoral staff coincided with a variety of new ministries and organizational changes, two issues would overshadow all others in the early years of the new millennium. As an 11-year member of the congregation, Bob Kettering was aware of two major challenges facing the church as he assumed his pastoral role. "Number one," he says, "contemporary worship. We were very traditional at the time. There wasn't much praise music or contemporary music." Second was the condition of the building. "The building was a beautiful building, but we were really hurting for space for adult Sunday school classes. And not much had been updated in the church for a long time."

"So I suppose I should have had my head examined," Bob reflects, "realizing that a building program and transitioning worship probably are two of the biggest pitfalls for any pastor. But those were the two things we had to deal with immediately."

Beginnings of a Building Project

What would grow into a $3.7 million building project began innocently enough with the appointment of a Feasibility Study Committee by the congregation in May 1998. Chaired by Marty Hershey, the committee was charged with examining church facilities, future programing and equipment needs, long-range staffing needs, and strengthening the congregation's stewardship commitment. Other committee members were Garth Becker, Bonnie Frey, Jim Hess, and Ron Martin. After a year of conversations and data gathering from staff and laity and various commissions and committees of the church, the committee presented its findings to the the congregation in May 1999. The report consisted of a comprehensive list of desired building improvements identified by the congregation. Topping the list was a "complete facelift of the church."

Specifics included nine additional adult classrooms; a bigger office suite; an enlarged narthex/gathering area with hospitality center; updated and expanded kitchen; improved sound system and acoustics in the large fellowship hall; updating and handicapped accessibility for the children's wing; accessible and modern bathrooms; air conditioning; an exterior storage/workshop area; technology upgrades in the sanctuary, classrooms, and offices; landscaping; additional parking; and more.

While the church was taking initial steps toward a major project, some items required immediate action. The Church Board in June 1998 authorized $30,000 from the capital improvement fund and the Property Commission budget to make "major repairs" in the near future, including replacing exterior wooden doors, wrapping soffits and facia with aluminum, replacing windows in the large fellowship hall, and painting the building's remaining exterior wood. Once these projects were completed, the capital improvement fund was largely depleted, leaving the congregation with few accumulated resources for a major building program.

At the recommendation of the Board, the church in May 1999 appointed a Facility Improvement Committee to further examine the daunting list of identified needs and bring a recommendation in November on a way forward. The committee of Freeman "Fritz" Blough, chair; Garth Becker; Jim Hess; Shirley Hunter; Cindy Martin; and Rodney Moseman recommended the appointment of a Building Committee, allocation of $7,500 to hire an architect to prepare a master plan, and appointment of a Capital Campaign Committee. The committee already had met with two potential firms who could assist with a capital campaign. The congregation received the report and authorized the Board to appoint a Building Committee. Initial committee members were Fritz Blough, chair; Garth Becker, vice-chair; Harry Badorf; Paul Bewley; Mike Enck; Marty Hershey; Jim Hess; Janet Savage; and Pastor Bob Kettering, *ex officio*. Harry and Mike eventually resigned from the committee and Ken Hess and Rodney Young were added.

The committee began meeting in January 2000 and enlisted the services of Robert Beers and Kristen Worley, of Beers, Schellaci, & Hoffman, Ltd., to help translate the laundry list of building needs into preliminary plans with a ballpark price. It was around this time that things began to get interesting. The committee reported to the Church Board in July that the church could have everything it wanted; all it would take was a six-phase plan with a total cost of $8.5 million. Just the first phase to address some of the more urgent needs would cost $4.35 million. Forty years earlier the congregation had built the whole church and bought a parsonage for $425,000 and a decade later added on a gym and a chapel for less than $200,000. But times had changed.

Understandably, the plan produced severe sticker shock and began the lengthy and sometimes contentious process of prioritizing needs and evaluating what scale of project the congregation could afford. What everyone agreed on was that the final number had to be significantly less than $8.5 million. In October 2000 the church meeting in Special Council approved several affirmations. The first was that the church is not ready to adopt the full comprehensive plan, and the second was that they do believe "the overall church building needs a facelift." The Building Committee was charged with developing a less pricy plan, with focus on general refurbishing, upgrading heating and cooling systems, additional classrooms and office space, and some technological enhancements. The Church Board was authorized to sell the former church parsonage at 546 West Second Avenue to generate cash for building, and the church as a whole was charged with praying and striving for unity as the project moved forward. A capital campaign would be initiated only after a more specific building plan was approved.

Previously, in June 1999, the congregation had authorized the Church Board to sell another former church parsonage on Becker Avenue when the lease with current tenants expired. The Becker Avenue property was settled on January 31, 2000, for $144,798, and the funds later were designated for the building fund. The sale of the Second Avenue property in 2001 generated an additional $110,000.

While the Building Committee went back to the drawing board, the church authorized the Stewardship Commission in May 2001 to appoint a Capital Fund Committee "to research funding options to accompany any building plans which would be authorized by future Council action."

Working from the architect's original preliminary plans and additional work done by Rodney Young, the committee brought revised plans to a September 2001 Special Council Meeting—this time with a $4 million cost estimate. The committee recommended breaking ground by March 1 on the project, which could be completed in two years or less.

At the same meeting the Stewardship Commission brought a proposal to hire John H. Miller of JHM Associates for $4,800 to conduct a feasibility study to take the congregation's pulse on the project and get a preliminary understanding of the level of financial support that could be expected. The feasibility study was approved by a unanimous vote and by a lesser margin the congregation also affirmed moving forward with schematic building plans, "subject to the availability of funds" to be determined by the study. At this point the church building fund had grown to $400,000, primarily through the sale of the former parsonages.

In November, JHM Associates reported the findings of the feasibility study, and the congregation approved the appointment of a committee to immediately launch a three-year capital campaign with a Victory Goal of $2 million and a Challenge Goal of $2.5 million. While not all of the building plans were solidified, the congregation gave the go-ahead for a site survey and storm water study and extensive renovations of the large fellowship hall. While the overall scope of the project and many of the details of the plan itself still were very much in question, this much was decided: The congregation would be building!

Named to the Campaign Committee were chair Mike Bingeman, Sue Bingeman, Edna Blymier, Jim Gibbel, Steve Hess, Dave and Susie Keim, Cindy Martin, Larry Sauder, and Mark Shelley. They reported in March 2002 that JHM Associates and People Spots consultant Jim Moss both were assisting with the campaign, which would begin in earnest in the fall under the banner of "Building Together That More May Know Him." By summer, the Bingemans had resigned from the committee. Larry Sauder was named chair and Robert Garner and Oren Spangenburg joined.

TIME CRUNCH

While the campaign planners needed more time to roll out the campaign, circumstances beyond the congregation's control were pushing them to move quickly. At a March 6, 2002, Special Council Meeting, Mike Enck reported that changes in the state building codes expected to be enacted in the summer could produce significant cost increases and delays in the project.

Still unsure of how much funding would be available, the church voted to submit master building plans to the Bureau of Labor and Industry before the changes would kick in. The congregation also affirmed Lebanon Building Systems—the company owned by Building Committee member Rodney Young—as the general contractor for the design/build project and set a $2.5 million goal for the financial campaign. With this budget, the church could complete site work, refurbish the entire building with updated mechanical systems and air conditioning, bring the existing building up to code, and add office space and five Sunday school rooms proposed in earlier plans. This was in addition to the large fellowship hall changes already approved.

The committee worked furiously over the spring and into summer to address concerns raised at the March Council and finalize a plan that would pass muster with the congregation, stay within budgetary limits, and beat the building code deadline. Points of contention included what some viewed as an excessive office suite and gathering area. Also under debate was a two-story educational wing that would be cost effective, but some thought diminished the architectural integrity of the building.

At a July 24, 2002, Special Council Meeting, the Building Committee presented a new $3,055,182 preliminary plan and the Capital Campaign Committee laid out its schedule for a fall campaign. Both were approved. While the plan still would undergo review by architects and need approval by Labor and Industry, the scope of the project now was clearly defined. It included about a million dollars for new construction, $1.5 million for refurbishing, and additional costs for site work, contingencies, and more.

Refurbishing included:
- Upgraded heating and cooling systems including central air conditioning throughout the building;
- Total upgrade of the entire facility to meet the requirements of the Americans with Disabilities Act;
- Expanded and upgraded restrooms;
- New paint, lighting, floor covering, and ceilings throughout the building (except sanctuary and chapel);
- New flooring, storage, sound proofing, and sound system in the large fellowship hall;
- A ramp to access the sanctuary stage; and
- A large gathering area and carport.

New construction included:
- A spacious gathering area and unloading canopy (carport);
- Tripling of office space and doubling the number of offices from four to eight;
- Doubling of the kitchen, including a walk-in refrigerator and freezer;
- More than 3,000 square feet of classroom space on the first floor, plus a youth and junior high room above the new kitchen and lavatories;
- A choir director's office and doubling the size of the choir room with a concrete roof for HVAC units; and
- Storage and maintenance space.

Not included in the cost estimate was any funding for furnishings or landscaping.

By October the Lead Gifts Phase of the Building Together campaign was completed, and the campaign goal had grown to $3.1 million to cover the cost of the project. When all campaign pledges were tallied in November, they came in short of the $2 million original goal ($1,886,000), but JHM Associates recommended that the church proceed in confidence that the project could be completed with manageable debt. Complicating matters, Rodney Young reported to the Board that Lebanon Building Systems was insolvent and filing for chapter 11 bankruptcy. The company would not be able to serve as general contractor, although he was willing to serve as Construction Manager.

With a vote of confidence for Rodney from the Building Committee—whose members would need to assume additional general contractor responsibilities—the Board agreed to recommend this arrangement to the church. Finally, at a November 17, 2002, Council Meeting the congregation voted 98-20 to move ahead with the building project, with a not-to-exceed cost of $3,055,182, and 105-17 to authorize the Stewardship Commission to obtain construction financing of up to $2 million. Both votes were well above the required two-thirds majority and a strong sign that the congregation was united. Made clear in the proposals was that not all expenses were covered in the $3.1 million figure and that a second capital campaign likely would be needed to retire $1.2 million of expected long-term debt. After four-and-one-half years of painstaking planning and preparation, the project was poised to begin. But there still were significant hurdles to be cleared.

Beginning in December, the Building Committee mobilized 16 sub-committees to help make the hundreds of decisions that would need to be made, and sub-contractor bids were solicited. The committee reported to the Board in late February 2003 that, though the state had not yet started requiring the new building code, Lititz borough had, effective January 1, creating a need to rework plans and adding $250,000 in additional expense, mostly for fire-related features. Had the congregation moved six months earlier, they could have saved a quarter million dollars.

Broken Ground and Busted Budgets

Around the beginning of April, excavation began and quickly came to a halt when two abandoned underground oil tanks were discovered. Cost to remove them? $10,000. A short time later a sinkhole scuttled plans. Cost to fill it? $12,000.

"Now we are $22,000 in the hole before we really get rolling here," Building Committee member Ken Hess recalls, plus the major cost increase from the building code changes. "It was a lot of extra money," says Fritz Blough. "We really weren't a very popular group for a while."

The good news was that a number of sub-contractor bids had come in lower than expected. At a May 2003 Council Meeting, Fritz Blough expressed confidence that the project still could be completed within the not-to-exceed amount, despite the early and significant setbacks. As of early June, the congregation still didn't have a building permit, but the borough was permitting preliminary site work. Permits finally were in hand by the end of July, but the project was behind schedule. Asbestos issues with flooring in the children's area and a second sinkhole caused further delays, but things were progressing out front with the new gathering area and office suite, and in the children's wing. By mid-August, the project was two months behind schedule, with the children's area expected to be completed in early November and the office suite soon after the first of the year. Then work would move to the adult educational wing, before wrapping up in the large fellowship hall in the rear. Meanwhile, Warwick High School was providing parking spaces for the church on Sundays and the pastors were banished to temporary modular office space behind the church. Once work would begin in the educational wing, Moravian Manor would provide space for Sunday school classes to meet for several months in 2003 and 2004.

Pastor Steve Hess fondly remembers the year several staff "lived" in the trailer on cinder blocks in the back parking lot. "When it would rain," he recalls with a laugh, "the water would come in on my desk." He would wipe it off and keep working. The décor in the temporary office was vintage trailer. Steve remembers one guest who stopped in and drolly observed that the only thing that's missing is a velvet picture of Elvis on the wall.

Complicating the work for the contractors and life for the church was the need to balance the ongoing ministries of the church with the construction work.

"The whole time we were doing the construction we were using this facility," notes Ken Hess. "Normally guys can work up until 4:30 or 5 o'clock and drop their tools and run. Well, they couldn't do that here. They had to do some cleaning up and policing the area because that night something was going on here." Ken recalls the workers, who had built other churches, observed the unusually high level of activity. While other churches may have had Wednesday night activities, something was going on at Lititz nearly every night of the week.

The project got a shot in the arm in October with the announcement that Lititz Meals on Wheels had won a grant of $20,800 from the Lancaster County Foundation to help fund the kitchen renovations. A newsletter article credited Oren Spangenburg for his work on the grant application and noted that the church had donated its facilities for some 30 years for use by Meals on Wheels. In 2014, the church website reported that more than one million meals had been served from the Lititz kitchen since 1973.

The congregation also was coming together to raise additional funds. Special events such as an April 2003 Precious Transfers Auction of donated items raised funds for furnishings. Later in the project, as individual members became aware of needs, they quietly donated to meet those needs. Some well-timed memorial gifts also helped piece the puzzle together. Furniture, kitchen appliances and accessories, bulletin boards,

Meals on Wheels volunteers prepare food in March 2013. More than a million meals have been prepared at the church for this program since 1973.

wallpaper, stained glass doors, a gathering area chandelier, and library furnishings were just some of the items donated by members. And other members donated their time to complete smaller tasks to finish up the project.

By the end of 2003 children's classrooms were again occupied, and work was progressing out front. In November the committee noted some additional unexpected expenses not covered by contingencies, such as replacing flat rubber roofs and buying a new security system—an addition of $22,000 in costs.

By March 2004, due to some unexpected items already mentioned above and additional change orders, it was clear that the project would exceed the $3.1 million not-to-exceed figure approved by the church, so the committee asked for and received approval for $455,000 of additional expenses, bringing the project total to $3.5 million.

The fact that the committee came to the church for permission after the funds were already earmarked evidently didn't sit well with some. In April, Stewardship Commission chair Jeff Tennis reported serious financial strains to the Board, as giving was well below budget, benevolences to outreach ministries were unpaid, and additional interest payments for the building project were scheduled to kick in in the coming year. The Commission brought seven recommendations aimed at implementing better controls on building project spending and making it clear that, going forward, any new expenses would need to be offset by cuts in other areas so that costs for the total project would go no higher. The Board threatened that these measures could lead to work stoppage if costs were not contained. And the Stewards also noted that no plan yet existed to fund furnishings for the new portions of the building.

Despite everyone's best efforts, they still weren't able to stop the bleeding. In July the Board brought one more recommendation to the church to allot an additional $225,000 to complete the project. (The final cost of the project came in at $3,736,485.91, another $11,000 beyond this final limit.) While costs were a serious concern, the church was beginning to enjoy the fruits of their labor and giving. By June 2004 the project was 80 percent complete. Still remaining was work in the back of the church in the kitchen, large and small fellowship halls, and additional youth classrooms. In the September *Observer*, the committee reported expected completion by the end of the month, but additional complications in receiving occupancy permits further delayed completion and resulted in postponement of the dedication service.

By year-end the 18-month project was completed. The facility was dedicated on April 10, 2005, during an open house that involved former pastors in a celebration of the church's 90th anniversary. Fritz Blough delivered the final report of the Building Committee to the May 18 Council Meeting, thanking other committee members for their hard work, the Capital Campaign Steering Committee for its efforts, the congregation for helping to shape the project through their participation in meetings and for backing it with their financial support and, ultimately, God for bringing the project to completion. Throughout the building process, even at its messiest times, Fritz frequently communicated the ways he saw God's hand at work. And he expressed faith that the Lord would continue to guide the Lititz Brethren as they faced ongoing debt challenges.

And while there had been serious debates and disagreements along the way over the size, style, and substance of the project, when it was completed nearly everyone agreed that the church once more had a beautiful, state-of-the-art facility that would serve them and the community well for decades to come.

"It was a trying experience at times," says Fritz Blough, "but it was the first time I ever did anything where I really felt I was using my talents to the fullest for something worthwhile."

One final touch to all the church improvements was completed in 2007. With a growing trend in the funeral industry toward cremation, members of the church envisioned a beautiful garden where cremains could be buried. The idea was first broached in spring 2004, but the Property Commission reported that zoning laws posed obstacles. After further research, ground was broken in September 2006, and the nearly completed garden was dedicated October 1. The 24-by-30-foot garden includes

300 one-square-foot grids for interment, five of which were put to use the first fall. A substantial donation from the estate of John Graybill, along with other donations and the efforts of Memorial Garden Committee members Gerald and Carol Kurl, Rodney and Verna Moseman, and Sarge and Toni Earhart, enabled the garden to be completed in just six months. A cross comprised of bricks dedicated to loved ones serves as a focal point.

Retiring Debt: "Our Church Came Through"

As the building project was wrapping up, the Board was addressing tight finances caused by a soft economy and accompanying reduction in giving to the church budget, along with the increased debt burden the church had assumed. In December 2004 the Board discussed how outreach giving to denominational and district ministries would be prioritized as funds would become available. At that point, none of the church's contributions for 2004 had been made. It was hard for some members of a church that had been known for its strong financial support of denominational ministries to not be able to meet commitments. It would take several years before support of denominational and district agencies would rebound.

In March 2005, at a Special Council Meeting the church approved hiring JHM Associates for $28,000 to assist with a second three-year capital campaign to continue to attack the building debt. As of June 2005, debt stood at $1,921,700, a portion owed to the bank and the rest in promissory notes issued to members. The new Campaign Committee of Oren Spangenburg, chair; Ethan Gibbel, secretary; Dave & Suzi Keim, financial recorders; Jim Gibbel; Carol Ludwig; Jim Ross; Larry Sauder; George Way; and, serving *ex officio,* Pastor Steve

A STITCH IN TIME RAISED $60,000

A surprisingly effective fundraising force was a group of women brandishing needles. An April 2005 *Observer* article noted that the quilters of the church had taken on a new name and a new mission. The name was the Golden Needles Club. The mission? Sewing to retire building debt. While this group of seamstresses previously had sewn mostly quilts and wall-hangings to sell at the annual Brethren Disaster Relief Auction, the article explained, "Working in our new facility has inspired us to do more than just quilting." They set up shop in the new media room in the church and began making table runners, placemats, and other small items to help retire building debt. Members of the group in 2006 included Helen Ament, Jean Bachman, Nancy Erwin, Ruth Groff, Joanne Hess, Jean Hoover, Annetta King, Erla Mae Levenson, Alverta Long, Joyce Sheaffer, Barb Showers, Janet Steffy, Reda Thomas, and Christina Wohlforth.

And stitch by stitch, they started making an impact. By September 2006, they already had raised nearly $10,000. At the two-year mark, profits exceeded $16,000. By December 2008, it was more than $30,000. A newsletter article observed, "This is amazing considering our highest priced item is $48." But the ladies continued to make attractive items and effectively market their creations at venues including the Disaster Relief Auction, the annual Lititz Craft Show, and at a little shop set up in the church. (And they continued to make quilts for disaster relief, as well.) By June 2010 profits had grown to $44,000, and by the end of the year $48,500. In a March 2011 *Observer* article on the final campaign, Jim Gibbel gave the Golden Needles a shout out. Noting that they now had raised $51,300, he wrote, "Their needles are certainly 'GOLDEN.'" According to one member, in about eight years the group eventually raised more than $60,000 to retire the debt.

DAUNTING CHALLENGES 171

The handiwork of the Golden Needles' sewing group generated $60,000 for the building fund. Ruth Groff (left) and Joanne Hess display a wall-hanging in 2013.

Hess and Board chair Henry Renn; set to work on the "Fulfill the Vision . . . Live the Mission" campaign, seeking three-year commitments from 2006 through 2008.

By November 2007, debt had been reduced to just over $1 million, and the congregation not only was giving generously through the campaign, but also in other ways. A dinner featuring the Jazz Ministers, sponsored by the Builders and Cornerstone Sunday school classes in April 2007 raised more than $40,000 for the building fund. In April 2009 an $800-per-table dinner featuring chicken cordon bleu and entertainment by local talent brought in an additional $43,000. A Guess Who's Coming to Dinner event in November 2009 raised nearly $17,000 more. During 2010 members used "grow money" to fund projects to raise money to retire debt. A December 2010 *Observer* article reported that nearly $20,000 had been raised by members creating items including marble chasers and other woodworking projects, paintings, frakturs, shoofly pies and other baked goods, special dog food, and more. Following the second campaign a Capital Gifts Committee, chaired by Earl Ziegler, was charged with working at reducing the debt through campaigns and other means. This committee spearheaded some of these special fundraising efforts.

By June 2010, the building debt had been reduced to $500,000, with the first campaign having generated about $1.86 million in gifts, the second $1.33 million, and additional giving and events accounting for the rest. Plans now were underway for a third campaign to wipe out the remaining debt with commitments for the latter part of 2010 through 2013. Chaired by Jim Gibbel, the "Celebrate the Journey" campaign resulted in pledges of $568,645. Carl Martin constructed a replica of the church steeple that was placed in the gathering area to track the disappearing debt in $25,000 increments. After years of sacrificial giving by the congregation, Capital Gifts Committee chair Earl Ziegler had the privilege of reporting in the church newsletter that as of October 16, 2012, the Lititz Church of the Brethren was entirely debt-free. Debt that had appeared to some as an insurmountable obstacle was retired in less than a decade.

"Our church came through," says moderator Jeff Glisson. "In the end, it was a positive thing. . . . The congregation stepped up and responded to that very strongly. This congregation has a history of responding to special emphases like building projects."

A celebration of the achievement was held on Sunday, December 3. Campaign pledges would continue to come in through 2013, with 75 percent designated for future building needs and the rest for outreach.

How Will We Worship?

While the building project dominated the first years of the new millennium, the second major issue was the addition of a contemporary worship service. In fact, the renovation of the large fellowship hall was specifically designed to create another area suitable for a worship service.

During the first quarter of 1999 recently installed Pastor Bob Kettering had met with 273 members in "cottage meetings" to get to know the church better and hear what was on people's hearts and minds. In an April *Observer* column, Bob noted that "one area that received a lot of discussion was worship; with several wanting more familiar, old-fashioned hymns and several expressing a desire for more contemporary worship. The area of worship," he concluded, "will prove to be the most challenging in the future as we try to meet the worship needs of a diverse congregation." Over time, the new pastor's prediction would prove prescient as worship services and schedules would become a point of contention for nearly a decade.

The addition of a contemporary worship service was not a new idea. It had been on the minds of some when what would become the chapel service began in 1995. The 10-year goals that grew out of the People Spots planning process specifically called for the initiation of a third worship service in 1999—although the goal didn't say what style the service should take and actually suggested it be held during the week to accommodate those unavailable on Sunday. But with the church in the midst of a staffing transition, in May 2000 the People Spots Committee recommended the additional service be put on hold until vacant staff positions were filled. The Executive Committee, it was reported, would put in place an *ad hoc* committee to study this goal, with the help of a consultant. The consultant ended up being Jim Moss, who had worked extensively with the congregation through People Spots. Providing additional impetus for a contemporary service was a 2001 request from the Disciples Sunday school class, comprised primarily of young adults.

The process of introducing contemporary praise choruses to a congregation accustomed to choirs and organs and led by a classically trained music staff got underway early in 2001 with the creation of a "worship team." Initially the team was utilized to lead music during special Sunday morning services like Youth Sunday and Children's Day and occasionally during the choir's summer off season. In addition, once a month the worship team led music for the mid-week Wednesday Nights ALIVE service.

In his October 2001 newsletter column Pastor Kettering

delicately broached the issue of musical styles. While affirming his own love of old hymns, he encouraged the congregation to "sing to the Lord a new song" (Ps. 96:1) and suggested that the Psalmist penned those words because he "knew that God's people would need to be pushed and prodded into singing new songs to the Lord." He then outlined several affirmations regarding music that the Worship and Fellowship Commission recently had agreed upon. Among them: 1) The worship team would continue to lead music on Wednesday nights and once a quarter in one of the Sunday worship services; (It was specifically noted that these services would be announced in advance—presumably so those who wanted to sing a new song could and those who didn't could choose the other service.) 2) The church remained committed to a traditional service relying primarily on organ, piano, and hymnal; 3) An upcoming sermon series by the pastors and an April 20, 2002, worship seminar led by Robert Webber would inform future discussions. Webber, at the time, was recognized as a leading national thinker and author on worship.

In the weeks following the Webber seminar, Jim Moss administered a "Worship Vision Questionnaire." The congregation gathered for a day-long seminar with Moss in September to review the results and continue to move toward introducing a contemporary worship service. At the November Council Meeting Worship and Fellowship Commission chair Jeff Glisson reported the results of the survey and seminar and received Council endorsement "to go forward with forming a committee to study options for a contemporary worship service." (It was a momentous meeting; the congregation also approved moving forward with the building project.) The minutes noted that Jim Gibbel urged the congregation to consider other options, including a blended service, a Taize service, or converting one of two existing services to contemporary. A concern from the start was that an additional service might spread the congregation too thin, leaving worshippers scattered among empty pews in the sanctuary. (And it was true that when the goal of a third service had been established, the congregation also had projected significantly higher attendance by the time a service would be added.) Despite concerns, the committee was approved, but with reassurance that any worship recommendations would require future Council approval.

Appointed to the Contemporary Worship Committee were chair Joel Gibbel, Michele Gibbel, Kim Glisson, Cindy Martin, Lynne Thompson, and Terry Zeiders; Ministry Commission representative Jim Wenger; youth representatives Gail Longenecker and Jonathan Shenk; and Pastor Kettering.

The committee presented a report in the form of questions and answers at the May 2003 Council Meeting, explaining how a contemporary service would be different, detailing some benefits of a contemporary service, and seeking to address concerns. The committee's thinking was becoming clearer. The new service likely would be held in the renovated large fellowship hall; might include testimonies, multi-media, and drama in addition to preaching and contemporary music; and could start early in 2004, depending on congregational approval and building project progress. The committee booked "praise teams" from four other congregations to lead worship during four summer services in preparation for a vote to be held at a Special Council in September.

Discussion was lengthy at the September 21 meeting, where the committee proposed:

- Implementing a contemporary service in fall 2004;
- Hiring a part-time staff member to coordinate music and worship for the new service and

reconfiguring the rest of the music staff upon Joan Fyock Norris' retirement; and
- A specific worship schedule.

Sensing the congregation disagreed with various parts of the proposal, Verna Moseman introduced an amendment gutting the proposal of many of the specifics, leaving only affirmation that a third service would be implemented in fall 2004, pending completion of the building project, staffing availability, and congregational support. Even with many of the controversial specifics punted down the road, the proposal to affirm having a contemporary worship service passed by a narrow 40-38 vote, portending future difficulties. Another soft vote to continue working on the service received stronger support (61-25) at the November Council Meeting, but the most vexing issue—the worship schedule—still lay ahead.

When Will We Worship?

The congregation met the schedule head-on at a March 14, 2004, Special Council Meeting. While the committee in the fall had proposed leaving the traditional 8 and 10:30 worship services and 9 a.m. Sunday school untouched, while adding an 11 a.m. contemporary service, by March they had a new schedule to propose: For seven weeks in the fall, put the 8 a.m. service on pause. Hold the contemporary service at 8:30, the traditional at 11, with Sunday school at 9:45. If support continued for the 8 a.m. service, it would resume October 31.

A proponent of the existing schedule proposed a substitute motion to leave the schedule alone and let the committee plan the contemporary service for whenever they wanted. After vigorous discussion, the substitute motion failed 64-48. A subsequent vote on the original motion passed 80-32.

At the May Council, Bob Kettering used his pastor's report to promote the coming contemporary service as a tool for outreach, while also seeking to reassure traditionalists. "Rest assured," he wrote, "we will not emphasize the contemporary worship service to the detriment of the traditional service." At the same meeting the Worship and Fellowship Commission reported that they expected to have a highly qualified Director of Worship Ministries in place as soon as June 1 to work with the new service and also a Director of Music Ministries to replace Joan Fyock Norris after her June 30 retirement. As part of the May 23, 2004, Music Celebration Sunday, the congregation thanked Joan for more than 20 years of service as Director of Music Ministries.

Assuming the role of Director of Worship Ministries in charge of coordinating the contemporary service was Ken Trovinger, who brought a music education degree and more than 10 years of experience leading worship, including time as Music Director at New Holland United Methodist Church. Replacing Norris as Director of Music Ministries in charge of the choir and men's chorus was Elizabethtown College graduate and Drexel University music faculty member Scott Bacon. Both were installed during the July 11 worship service.

Because the large fellowship hall renovations weren't complete, the new contemporary service kicked off on Sunday, September 12, 2004, in the church sanctuary with attendance of 260. Traditional service attendance that Sunday was 185. The addition of the new service produced an initial surge in overall attendance, with average attendance for the first four weeks of the new schedule 60 people above the previous year.

Later in the fall the contemporary service moved to the large fellowship hall.

But the issue of the early traditional service remained. While some may have thought the service would go away after the seven-week hiatus, they were wrong. A strong core group remained committed and early worship resumed on October 31. In December, by Board action the service was relocated to the chapel and the starting time pushed back to 8:15.

At the May 2005 Council Meeting, Music and Worship Commission chair Jeff Glisson reported that since the new schedule kicked in on September 12, the 8:30 contemporary service averaged 145 attendees, the 11 a.m. traditional service in the sanctuary, 170, and (since its October 31 reinstatement) the 8:15 a.m. chapel service was averaging 55, for a combined attendance of 370. Despite major attention focused on meaningful worship services designed to cater to people of various tastes, overall attendance remained stubbornly flat and by 2008 would begin a steady decline. And people still were unhappy with the schedule. Eight-thirty was too early for a contemporary service attended mostly by younger people and 11 a.m. worship made for a late lunch for those attending the traditional service. Some also felt that worshiping at widely disparate times produced a greater sense of fragmentation in the congregation. Alas, the schedule approved in spring 2004 had included a provision for re-evaluation by the end of 2005.

During the fall months, the Worship Service Schedule Evaluation Team issued a survey to gauge feelings about the worship schedule and received an eye-popping 312 returned surveys, but no clear direction. In November, Council agreed to continue with the current schedule, but test an alternative schedule with the congregation in coming months: 8 a.m. chapel service, 9:15 Sunday school, and concurrent traditional and contemporary services at 10:30.

This resulted in more surveying in early 2006 to get input on the two competing schedules. Other than a growing sentiment that all the surveying was getting a little tiresome, no consensus emerged. The committee reported that the 245 surveys were split nearly equally between the two plans. With no clear direction from the congregation, the committee recommended to the May 2006 Council Meeting that no change be made in the schedule. Council rejected the recommendation and asked the Board to come up with a better option. With King Solomon unavailable to help, the task was handed back to the committee, some of whose members changed along the way. The committee asked for more time in spring and fall 2007. Toward the end of 2007 they did another round of surveys and in February 2008 brought a recommendation to the Board, which was approved, before being rescinded in April. The Board decided to hold another round of hearings on various proposals, and put the question to the congregation once and for all at the May Council Meeting.

The new schedule proposed to the church in May maintained the chapel service at 8:00, followed by Sunday school at 9:00, coffee and fellowship from 10:00 to 10:30, traditional worship at 10:15 and contemporary at 10:30, which would enable the pastor to more easily preach in the traditional service and join the contemporary service in progress to preach again.

After three-and-a-half years of dissatisfaction with the schedule implemented in fall 2004, after multiple surveys and discussions, after many of the congregation's best leaders had leant their keenest thinking to the issue for years, the revised schedule was presented to the congregation in May 2008. It was voted down 67-65. The schedule remained unchanged.

The issue continued to fester for two more years and ultimately was unable to be addressed by a congregational vote. Instead, a Vision Team appointed in fall 2008 to work alongside consultant Craig Sider in setting vision for the congregation quietly addressed the matter as part of its larger work. A May 2010 cover story in the *Observer* reported that the Church Board had affirmed a recommendation from the Vision Team to implement a new worship schedule, effective June 13. Without congregational vote, the chapel service was eliminated, the traditional service was moved to 9:00 a.m., followed by the contemporary at 9:15, fellowship time/continental breakfast beginning at 10:00, and Sunday school from 10:30 to 11:30. It was noted that this proposal would address nearly all of the concerns with the previous schedule. The biggest cost was the offense caused to the devotees of the chapel service.

Pastor Kettering in his June newsletter column pleaded with the congregation to get on board with the new schedule: "After three separate committees have tried to set the times for worship for our congregation," he wrote, "the visioning team made a fourth attempt. The new schedule may not be perfect, not everyone will see it to their liking . . . , but can we unite as a congregation around the new schedule for worship and Sunday School and focus on what really matters to God . . . not the time or style of our worship but making sure our hearts are really ready to worship and adore the Lord our God?"

The Vision Team provided additional rationale for the new schedule in their report to the November Council Meeting: "This change was made to create a greater spirit of congregational unity with two rather than three services. This change also allows for more flexibility, creativity, and lay participation in worship and better use of worship resources."

The Music and Worship Commission evaluated the new schedule at the end of 2010 and reported "that we have lost some regular attendees due to the early start of the services." Nevertheless, the schedule implemented in June 2010 remains in place at this writing and surveys and new schedule proposals have ceased, at least for now.

The Lititz congregation wasn't alone in its struggles to adopt new forms of worship and music. Bob Kettering knew, coming in, that such changes seldom came easily, and more than one congregation had experienced division. The term "worship wars"—used by some to describe conflict over musical preferences—didn't arise out of a vacuum. But few could have predicted that the simple matter of devising a satisfactory Sunday morning schedule would create so many years of debate and dissatisfaction. Members are reticent to offer explanations of how the relatively mundane matter of scheduling service times could become so contentious. Perhaps, voting on the schedule became the way that some members expressed dissatisfaction with the overall direction of segmenting the congregation into separate services based on music and worship preferences. While the church was able to accommodate those desiring more contemporary worship, those in the traditional service were left to adjust to emptier pews and what some felt to be a diminishing of the church's central service.

Renewed Refugee Resettlement

While significant energy and resources were dedicated to the building project and changes in worship, the rest of the church's ministries were far from static. In fact, the church remained extremely active in a variety of outreach and service projects close to home and around the world.

In 2002 the congregation renewed its long-standing commitment to resettling refugees. More than a decade had passed since they had assisted the Bilik family transition from Russia to the Lititz area. Twelve years later they were ready to help another Russian family. Vladimir and Luba Mironov, their son Vladimir and daughters Irina and Tanya arrived on April 10, and were settled into the same Liberty Street home that Jean de Perrot had offered for the previous refugee family. With family members already living in the community, the Mironovs had a support network in place, but still there was plenty for the church to do. Witness Commission chair Lisa Krieg in a May newsletter article acknowledged the de Perrots and many people who

The Lititz Brethren sponsored the Johnny family, from Burma, in 2008. Pictured here in June 2008 are (from right) Diamond and Angel and children Fairy, Honey Dew, and Bush Canary. The Johnnys and their relatives, the Shee Sho family, have become actively involved in the congregation.

gave time, money, and furnishings to make the house on Liberty Street a home. At the May 2003 Council Meeting the Witness Commission report also thanked church members who provided transportation, helped the Mironovs find jobs, and assisted the children as they began school. The Mironovs, the report said, "were very appreciative of all the help they received."

In 2008, the congregation welcomed two new refugee families—this time from the southeast Asian country of Myanmar, also known as Burma. After decades of persecution that many considered ethnic cleansing by the government in Myanmar, more than a half-million members of the Karen ethnic group—many of whom were Christian—were displaced within their country or in refugee camps along the border with Thailand. Beginning in 2005, governments around the world began to accept Karen people from the camps for permanent resettlement, with the United States accepting the largest number. Church World Service in Lancaster was a key agency in this resettlement effort. Additional refugees from Chin State in Burma also were included.

In April the Lititz congregation learned of the need for churches to resettle Burmese refugees, and that a number of churches in Lititz already were involved. In June the Board approved a recommendation from the Witness Commission to join the effort, if volunteers and funding could be found. They could, and on June 17 the first of three Karen families that the congregation would assist arrived. Diamond and Angel Johnny had lived the previous 18 years in a refugee camp. Their three children, Fairy, 13, Honey Dew, 10, and Bush Canary, 6, had known no other life. With help from the church they set up housekeeping in a second floor apartment at 301 S. Broad Street. Garth & Helen Becker and Kitty Hackman provided whole rooms of furniture to furnish the apartment.

On September 10, a second family arrived. Shee Sho was the brother of Diamond Johnny. Their families had lived together for eight years in the refugee camp and were happy to be reunited on American soil. The Shee Sho family included Shee and his wife, Bway Hser Ku; son Poe Kwar Hsee, 10; and daughters Mu Mu, 8, and Ester Shee, 6. They moved into a second floor apartment at 118 N. Liberty Street. Both the Johnnys and Shos were professionals; Diamond was a Community Health Educator and Angel a science teacher, while the Shos both were trained nurses. Both families began attending the church and quickly became part of the church family. (Later, when sponsorship by another church broke down for a third family in the community, the Lititz Brethren also supported Poe Chi and six family members.)

Heading up the resettlement effort from the congregation were coordinators Verna Moseman and Joan Gibbel. Other team members responsible for various tasks were Kitchen/Bathroom, Phylllis Martin; Bedroom/Living Room, Renee Child; Education, Carol Kurl, Linda Saylor; Clothing, Elaine Gibbel; Medical Needs, Dr. Bill Longenecker; Transportation, Ralph Moyer, Carl Martin; and Housing/Employment, Jim Gibbel, Earl Ziegler. Dozens of members contributed money and items, assisted with transportation, and befriended the new members of their community. More than 20 Lititz Brethren assisted with transportation to language classes and other appointments, and five tutored the children in English during the summer months.

In October, the Witness Commission reported to the Church Board that recently 66 Burmese had attended a worship service at Lititz, with a time of fellowship following the service. By summer 2009, Diamond Johnny and Shee Sho reportedly were working 30 hours per week at Lititz Family Cupboard Restaurant, and continued to search for full-time work. The Johnnys had completed language training and the Shos were continuing their studies. Eighth-grader Fairy Diamond was recognized at a special ceremony as an honor student, despite having not spoken any English a year earlier. Church member Nancy Leed was credited for tutoring Fairy throughout the year.

Youth lead worship at a June 2013 Karen worship service in the Lititz Chapel.

On March 28, 2010, Diamond, Angel, and Fairy Johnny and Shee and Bway Sho became members of the church by reaffirmation of faith. Fairy also was baptized. Witness Commission chair Earl Ziegler reported to the Board in December 2010 that both families were self-supporting, with the exception of needing help to purchase cars. Deepening their ties to the Karen/Chin Community, Lititz hosted its first Karen language community worship service on July 25, 2013, and settled into a pattern of an afternoon service the last Sunday of each month. Led by leaders of the local Karen community, the services attracted around 100 worshippers in the early months.

Going Into the World

While the Lititz Brethren were welcoming refugees into their community, they also were reaching out in the U.S. and abroad. In many ways, the first decade of the new millennium was a golden era of service, as members served multiple times in Louisiania, Haiti, the Dominican Republic, and places closer to home. Fueling the congregation's participation in mission across the U.S. and abroad was the fund established from the Irvin estate to support missions. Pastor Bob Kettering and Earl Ziegler also would serve on the seven-member Mission Advisory Committee for the denomination and on the Board of Brethren World Mission, further deepening the church's ties to overseas missions. Earl was a regular organizer of mission trips for groups in the Atlantic Northeast District.

In a January 2000 newsletter article reflecting on the previous year, Bob Kettering listed "commissioning several people to serve in mission projects around the world" among his highlights. Janice Gibbel, who had begun a two-year term with Brethren Volunteer Service (BVS) in October 1998 was serving at the L'Arche Community in Kilkenny, Ireland. Other members of the congregation performing long term volunteer assignments in the U.S. or abroad during the 1990s and 2000s included Kirsten Crosby, Ethan Gibbel, Wendi Hutchinson, Angela Oetama, and Nicole Oetama.

A single *Observer* issue in December 2000, highlighted a recent medical mission trip to Haiti by Dr. Bill & Betsy Longenecker and Gail & Rick Longenecker; Jim Eby's mission trip to Nicaragua; and Larry & Nancy Fittery's growing involvement with Keiyo Soy Ministries, which focused on providing clean drinking water in Kenya. From 2003 to 2005 Nancy Steedle served through BVS and the denomination's Global Mission Partnerships office at the Women's School of Ekklesiyar Yan'uwa a Nigeria (EYN—the Church of the Brethren in Nigeria), located at EYN headquarters near Mubi.

During the late 1990s and 2000s the congregation also was active locally with Habitat for Humanity, assisting in area building projects and supporting the organization through participation in an annual banquet. In June 1998, Lititz provided lunch and drinks for 100 volunteers participating in an area "Blitz Build" for Habitat. In December 2009, the Witness Commission reported that Gordon Mummaw had coordinated a team of nine volunteers from Lititz to help finish a Habitat house in Lancaster.

During the latter half of the 2000s, the Lititz Brethren spearheaded a major renovation of the Brooklyn (New York) First Church of the Brethren building and attached parsonage. In 2004, the congregation learned that the Brooklyn building was in dire need of deferred maintenance and renovations including a near total rewiring and repointing of the exterior walls. The estimated price tag was $150,000 to $180,000. Churches of the Atlantic Northeast District were being asked to pitch in to meet the need. None did more than Lititz. Working in partnership with the district, Lititz members Carl Martin, Gordon Mummaw, Ken Hess, and Earl Ziegler spearheaded the project. An anonymous donor from the district gave $60,000 and challenged others to match it. By January 2009, Lititz members had given more than $43,000 to help their sister church in New York City.

In 2012 Lititz members joined in a new community-wide effort to meet local needs. A program of the Lititz Ministerium coordinated by Love INC., The Lititz Project matched volunteers from local churches with area residents who needed help with projects such as home repairs. In 2013, groups from the congregation completed five projects, and the church was gearing up to participate again in 2014.

The Lititz Brethren also were quick to respond to needs when natural disasters struck. On December 26, 2004, a 9.0 magnitude earthquake in the depths of the Indian Ocean generated the most destructive tsunami in history, causing major damage and loss of life in 11 Asian countries. During January many individuals from the church and community purchased items and assembled 200 health kits for Church World Service to use to respond to the disaster, while also contributing $4,200 to the Church of the Brethren Emergency Disaster Fund.

When Hurricane Katrina devastated New Orleans and much of the southern United States in August 2005, the church quickly gathered $13,734 in cash, plus 41 blankets and 119 health kits to relieve victims' suffering and help with the recovery. But the immediate response was just the beginning. Brethren Disaster Ministries established long-term rebuilding projects along the Gulf Coast, including one in Chalmette, in St. Bernard Parish, Louisiana, in 2007. Over the next four years, a steady stream of Brethren volunteers wearing the signature red caps—2,141 in all—would stream into Louisiana to help rebuild homes. Among them were four teams from the Lititz congregation. The third one in March 2010 included 19 volunteers led by Ted Shotzberger. The final Lititz trip was in March 2011.

Meanwhile, another major disaster had struck further south. In fall 2008, Hurricanes Faye, Gustav, Hanna, and Ike had pounded Haiti. Heavy rains, mud slides, and raging rivers destroyed homes. In response, the Church of the Brethren began a modest home rebuilding effort. When an earthquake destroyed much of Haiti's capital Port-au-Prince on January 12, 2010, the Church of the Brethren was already on the ground and in position to partner with Haitian Brethren to launch one of its largest international disaster responses in decades. At the heart of the response was a home-building effort that resulted in 42 solid three-room homes after the hurricanes, and 78 more in response to the earthquake.

The Lititz Brethren had been serving in Haiti for more than a decade prior to the earthquake disaster—in fact a group of volunteers from Lititz was in Haiti just three days prior to the quake, working with the non-denominational Feed My Sheep Ministry (FMS) in Montrouis. Beginning in the mid-1990s, Dr. Bill and Betsy Longenecker and others had traveled annually to Haiti to engage in medical missions. Over time, the Longeneckers and Lititz Brethren had formed a relationship with FMS and its directors Richard and Beverly Felmey. In response to the 2008 storms and 2010 earthquake some members stepped up their commitment to FMS, a Christian ministry that included a vocational school, agricultural programs, a medical clinic, and church. In January 2009, the Longeneckers led a group of 11 college-age volunteers—including their sons

A September 2010 mission trip to Haiti included builders and sewers. Above in their red Brethren Disaster Ministries t-shirts and caps are (front) Earl Ziegler, Cheryl Garner, Earl Mull, (back) Ken Hess, Nancy Wenger, Carl Martin, John Knepp, Harold Hershey, and Jim Eby. (Mull and Knepp are members of other Brethren congregations.) Below Lititz member Nancy Wenger teaches sewing to eager students.

Billy and Bobby and Mark Risser and Natasha Blymier from the Lititz congregation—on a week-long trip to FMS. The team was able to take $12,500 in cash above what was needed for expenses, along with 26 suitcases filled with clothing, and medical, school, and health supplies. The following year, donations for the trip that ended three days before the quake totaled $16,650. Immediately after the quake the congregation channeled additional resources for relief to FMS.

At the same time the church was plugging in to Church of the Brethren rebuilding efforts. A January 23 trip to help build one of the "100 Homes for Haiti" that Brethren Disaster Ministries had committed to was quashed by the quake. The trip was rescheduled for September 13-19, 2010, when denominational staff member Jeff Boshart led Lititz members Jim Eby, Cheryl Garner, Harold Hershey, Ken Hess, Carl Martin, Nancy Wenger, and Earl Ziegler, along with two volunteers from other congregations. The group built a roof and installed doors on the Gonaives Church of the Brethren, installed hurricane clips on houses to anchor roofs during future storms, installed electricity in several homes, and also provided training in sewing. A grant of $4,000 from the church's Mission Fund covered building costs. Nancy Wenger taught sewing on two electric sewing machines donated by Nancy Erwin to 15 eager students. Using fabrics donated by the Golden Needles, and powering the machines with Pastor Romy's car battery, Nancy led each woman in creating a cloth bag with shoulder strap and a skirt or dress.

The Lititz church also served on the other half of the island of Hispaniola in the Dominican Republic. In January 2004 Bill and Betsy Longenecker spent a week in the Dominican Republic, working alongside Church of the Brethren Dr. Silhi Ricardo at nine different medical clinics. The congregation contributed thousands of dollars to buy medicines for Dr. Ricardo's ongoing work. Earl Ziegler led two groups that included some Lititz members to the Dominican Republic in February/March 2012 and December 2013 to help with church construction in Sabana Torsa and La Descubierta, respectively. The youth group also participated in a work camp in the Dominican Republic in 2013.

Excellence in Music

While the church was adding contemporary music to its repertoire during the early 2000s, it also was maintaining its reputation for excellence in music in general. Contributing to the church's ongoing interest in music has been Pastor Kettering, who himself is an accomplished musician. In anticipation of future organ needs, in July 1999, the Board approved the establishment of an organ fund that would continue to grow over the next decade.

In 2002, the church entered into a partnership with its neighbor—the Moravian Manor retirement community—to sponsor a new concert series. The community concert series, dubbed Music at Mid-Month, got underway in March 2002, featuring the J.P. McCaskey High School Gospel Choir. Other performers the first year included the piano/flute duet Cindy Wittenberg and Tracy Dietrich, and the Rockingham Male Chorus. Held several times a year, the Sunday afternoon concerts are provided as a free service to the community.

By 2010, the organ fund was growing and momentum was building for significant expansion of the church organ. The Music and Worship Commission was in discussion with the Walker Technical Company and proposed to the Board in February 2012 that $159,000 be dedicated to organ improvements, significantly more than the $123,000 in the organ fund. They decided to continue to raise funds. By April, the fund had grown and the commission had signed a contract to do what available funds allowed, while still seeking additional funding for midi, recording capability, and antiphonals, plus $1,200 in sanctuary modifications to close up the pit where the old console was located. A $7,900 contribution from the Elsie Hollinger estate during the summer months finally put them over the top, providing full funding for all options of the organ renovation. The work was completed in August, and on December 2, 2012, Dr. Ross Ellison played the dedicatory organ recital. According to a newsletter article announcing the recital, the new pipe and electronic organ, built by Walter Gundling and Robert Walker, featured four manuals with 87 ranks of stops, plus a built-in midi, "making it one of the finest, most versatile and largest organs in Lancaster County."

To showcase the instrument on an ongoing basis, early in 2013 the church initiated the Tuesday Tunes concert series, featuring local and guest organists in half-hour afternoon organ concerts the second Tuesday of each month.

YOUTH RENOVATION

Also new in the early years of the new millennium was the hiring of a youth pastor. In March 2003, the congregation approved seeking a full-time youth pastor. James Koser was named Director of Youth Ministries in July 2003, but his tenure was short-lived. Responsibility for youth was shifted to Pam Reist, who helped guide a strong youth group until her departure in 2008.

Debbie Evans joined the staff as Director of Christian Nurture on June 23, 2008, bringing 27 years of experience in Christian education, with previous employment at Highland Presbyterian Church and Hempfield United Methodist Church, and current service as Adjunct Professor of Religion/Humanities at Alvernia and Gwynedd Mercy Colleges. But youth were not included in her job description, leaving a void. With no staff assigned to the youth, lay members provided leadership, but felt they needed support from professional staff.

In April 2009, Bob Kettering proposed a major realignment of responsibilities among existing pastoral staff to free him to dedicate time to the youth. Over the next two years Bob cut back on teaching adult classes, attended fewer meetings, and preached one less time per month. Steve Hess and Debbie Evans took on additional responsibilities to allow for the shift.

Bob committed to visit all youth one-on-one, participate in their Sunday school class and activities, give greater visibility to youth in worship, personally recruit youth leaders, and "give input and coordinate the entire youth program of the church." In addition, he vowed to attend the 2010 National Youth Conference with the youth. As part of the efforts to beef up the youth ministry, the youth room underwent an extreme makeover in 2011, including new paint, furniture, juice bar, and large screen television. But when Bob's time with the youth came to a close, a new plan had not yet been formulated.

Concerned members tried to address the youth leadership void at the November 2010 Council Meeting by inserting a $30,000 line item in the church budget for a part-time youth pastor, but the church said "no" due to cost concerns. When Bob concluded his term with the youth in summer 2011, the congregation unsuccessfully sought an interim Coordinator of Youth Ministry from within the congregation. Instead staff responsibilities were reshuffled to allow Debbie Evans to become Interim Youth Ministry Coordinator to work with a team tasked with restructuring youth ministry.

The church had appointed a five-member Youth Renovation Team to study ways to provide leadership and reinvigorate the church's youth ministry. The team contracted with a consultant from Youth Ministry Architects to hold a round of listening sessions with youth, parents, church leaders, and others to assess the needs and potential of youth ministry at Lititz and determine leadership needs.

The results were compiled by mid-2011 in a 38-page report that included "recommendations for building a sustainable and growing youth ministry." Youth staffing wouldn't be entirely resolved until 2013, when Debbie would resign to take a position with the Lancaster County Council of Churches and would be replaced by part-time Director of Youth Ministries Jeffrey Keller and part-time Director of Children's Ministries Janet Myers.

While the church was revamping its own youth ministries with the new name iGNITE, it also opened its doors to a community youth ministry in February 2012. In September 2011, the Church Board had approved a proposal to host a TNT (Teens Need Truth) Youth Center, under the direction of Mike Wenger. The original TNT had begun in 2000 at Ephrata Mennonite Church, and leaders were looking to replicate the successful ministry in other communities. TNT's goal is to work and serve alongside the local schools and churches to reach out to youth and see lives transformed by Jesus Christ. The program includes interaction with students in schools during the day and a weekly evening gathering at the host church. Initially, Lititz hosted a TNT group for middle school-age youth on Monday night and for high schoolers on Tuesday, before settling into just Tuesday night each week. A few Lititz members joined the cadre of volunteers that staffed the program.

By 2014 TNT programs were hosted by Akron Church of the Brethren, Alive Church in Ephrata (formerly Ephrata Mennonite), Mohler Church of the Brethren, Bowmansville Mennonite Church, and Lititz, where about 50 junior and senior high youth attend a weekly "fun night" at the church.

Protecting Children

While Debbie Evans was asked to work with youth for a time, and also took on other responsibilities such as strengthening the church's public relations efforts, her central focus was the children's ministries of the church. When volunteers were not forthcoming for the 2010 summer Vacation Bible School, Debbie stepped in to keep the longstanding children's outreach going. By the following summer, with the approval of the Christian Education Commission, she had forged a partnership with Julie Campbell, her counterpart at nearby Hosanna Christian Fellowship, to offer a cooperative VBS. Hosanna hosted in 2011 and 2013 and Lititz in 2012, with both churches providing volunteers. In 2014, instead of Bible School, Lititz offered a new "Summer Kidz ALIVE" program on eight Wednesday evenings throughout the summer, while Hosanna returned to hosting its own VBS.

Child protection became a special emphasis during Debbie's tenure. Lititz had been an early adopter of basic child protection practices. A policy adopted in 2002 had implemented basic safeguards and expanded the congregation's understanding of child abuse. But it had stopped short of requiring crimi-

Elaborate artwork by Nancy Compton and a team of volunteer artists transformed the hallway walls in the children's wing in recent years.

nal background checks for staff and volunteers who worked with children. Soon after she arrived on staff in 2008, Debbie encouraged the congregation to take it to the next level. She explained in a July 2012 *Observer* column, "When I came here and found that we were not doing background checks, it was necessary to begin a new phase of the child protection process." After two years of education and preparation, background checks were approved.

In 2011, the congregation accepted an invitation from the Samaritan Counseling Center to be one of eight churches to participate in a year-long, grant-funded study of child abuse protection and the writing of handbooks to guide congregations. Debbie, along with Children's Ministry Coordinator Tonia Trovinger and Child Protection Coordinator Pam Martin, represented Lititz in this Safe Church Project, receiving 25 hours of education through monthly Saturday morning cohort meetings and intensive homework. In addition, Linda Crockett, the therapist heading the project, twice gave presentations to the congregation on the dangers of abuse and how to recognize it and prevent it, while also shielding adults from false accusations and limiting the church's liability. The Safe Church Project culminated with the Board's approval of a new Child Protection Policy and Handbook in June 2012.

While the new policy limited access to the children's wing of the church to protect children, another effort headed by artist Nancy Compton was making the children's wing much more inviting. During 2011 and 2012 Nancy and volunteers from the church and the Warwick High School art department painted a series of elaborate murals on the hallway walls of the children's wing, transforming plain institutional walls into scenes from storybooks. Scenes included trees, flowers, stone walls, wooden fences, birds and butterflies, a dog in a doghouse, a warm fireplace, and more.

New Vision, New Structure

The Vision Team that posed the winning solution to the worship schedule conundrum had been appointed at the initiative of Bob Kettering, who noted in a July 2008 proposal that initiating long-range planning was part of his position description. The Board already had been in conversation with Church of the Brethren Congregational Life Team Coordinator Stan Dueck about his possible involvement in developing a strategic plan, and Dueck would prepare a demographic study of the community to guide the work of the Vision Team. Later in the year a Vision Team was appointed. Members were chair Peggy Kammerer, Jenn Balmer, Joel Gibbel, Jeff Glisson, Cindy

Martin, Earl Ziegler, along with staff members Bob Kettering, Steve Hess, and Debbie Evans. An April 2009 newsletter article reported that the committee had employed former Brethren in Christ bishop and Infocus Leadership consultant Craig Sider to guide the group in formulating a Strategic Pathways plan. During 2009 the committee developed and tested with the congregation a new Vision Statement: "Transformed by Christ, Radically Loving, Living to Serve." The accompanying sentence stated, "Our vision is to be a Community where people are continually being transformed by Christ. People in this journey of transformation love radically and live to serve."

The team fleshed out the Vision Statement with four Strategic Initiatives, which were further broken down into 14 Key Goals. The four initiatives were on making disciples, worship, leadership, and outreach:

- To create a culture that encourages spiritual transformation and growth as disciples of Christ;
- To create a contagious worship environment that is authentic, engaging and invites participation of all persons in glorifying God;
- To call leaders and create a structure of leadership that is permission-giving, clear and dynamic in encouraging spiritual growth and ministry;
- To create a connected community of believers who live out their love of God by serving others and sharing the good news of Jesus Christ.

The team clearly understood its work to be sweeping. In a March 2010 *Observer* article committee member Joel Gibbel explained, "Everything is on the table. Programs may change, worship may change, leadership may change, and opportunities to serve may change."

On April 2, 2011, the Vision Team participated in a half day workshop with members of the Board, and a week later sent a letter to the Board urging immediate action on four items that grew out of the workshop: 1) Focus on the future, not on the past, as the church embraces "Jesus and his ministry for us," while shifting stewardship and budgeting away from a business model; 2) Appoint a task team to develop a new plan of organization that is streamlined, vision-driven, "missional," and encourages spiritual growth and ministry; 3) Appoint another task team to develop a staffing plan for growth that includes staff of various ages and focuses on reaching the dominant demographic groups in Lititz—those 0-16 and 30-55; and 4) Enhance the congregation's communication by embracing technology and social media and appointing a volunteer Communications Coordinator from within the congregation.

The most significant change to result from the Strategic Pathways planning process at this writing was the adoption of a new organizational plan, effective January 1, 2013. This part of the strategic plan was delegated to a Vision Structure Committee, comprised of Todd Christophel, Lauren Krak, Carol Kurl, Jim Weidemoyer, and Earl Ziegler. In an October 2011 report to the Church Board, the committee outlined what they hoped to achieve through the proposed organizational changes:

- The church needs to be structured around its mission, vision, and core values in an "intentional structure that is Spirit-led, prayer-based and mission-focused;"

- A simpler structure is needed that frees people "to do" ministry. Too much time is spent sitting in administrative meetings;
- Members need to be called to ministries for which they have passion. More opportunities are needed for people to use gifts in ministry, rather than meetings;
- A "permission-giving" culture is needed to allow people to initiate and carry out projects that are in harmony with the church's vision/mission; and
- More emphasis on short-term commitments, since that is the cultural trend.

Brian Rice, who served as the congregation's final Board chair in 2012 and became the first Leadership Team chair in 2013, described the old model: "You know, we come up with an idea. We have to bring it to the next group. They talk about it, send it back. Finally they vote on it. Then it goes to the congregation and they vote on it and maybe a year-and-a-half later we can actually do it. That's how it had always run, and that's what we're trying to get away from."

Vision Team member Joel Gibbel observes that the perception was, "Nothing gets changed around here because our structure is cumbersome. A permission-giving culture was what we were going for." While the church had tinkered with its organization a number of times through the years, the changes proposed by the Vision Structure Committee were perhaps the most significant since the elimination of the Official Board in the 1950s. It brought not only new nomenclature, but also represented an attempt to significantly alter the congregation's leadership culture.

While the Council Meeting (now named Congregational Meeting), comprised of all active members, remained in place as the highest authority, the 22-member Church Board, the smaller Executive Committee, and the Ministry Commission all were eliminated, replaced by an eight-member Leadership Team comprised of the senior pastor, moderator, church clerk, and five members called by the congregation. Instead of the congregation electing a Board chair, the Leadership Team would call its own chair from within its ranks. The Leadership Team not only would assume most of the responsibilities of the former Church Board, but also would supervise all paid staff, instead of having individual staff report to various commissions.

In the new structure, commissions were out, with six "Action Teams" replacing the seven commissions. Implicit in the name "Action Team" was that these bodies were empowered to act within the parameters of the church mission/vision without having to seek permission from the Leadership Team. The days of running proposals from committee, to commission, to Executive Committee, to Church Board, to Council (with occasional detours to address issues that arose) were to be a thing of the past. The Action Teams, comprised of five or more members each, included Christian Education, Fellowship & Hospitality, Stewardship of Property, Stewardship of Finance, Witness & Outreach, and Music & Worship. No members of these teams served on the Leadership Team.

While the change to a smaller Leadership Team was couched in terms of efficiency and relieving people of the burden of attending meetings, it also excluded some who may not have been looking for fewer meetings. Losing representation in the transition from Board to Leadership Team was the Deacon Board chair, church treasurer, and all pastoral staff other than the senior pastor. Also new, all pastoral staff members now would report to the senior pastor, who would be recognized as "the spiritual and executive leader."

While the goals of the new plan were clearly stated, the new structure also represented a pronounced concentration of power in the hands of the Leadership Team and senior pastor. In the congregation's earliest days most decisions were made by the church as a whole. By the 1950s, power was gravitating to a large Church Board, led by a chair elected by the congregation, which increasingly handled the day-to-day matters of the church. In 2003 the size of the Board had been reduced from more than 40 members to about 20. Now the senior pastor and seven elected members would wield considerable decision-making authority. In an interview, Moderator Jeff Glisson acknowledged the legitimacy of concerns about concentration of power, noting that it was something that would need to be monitored and could be helped through strong communication from the Leadership Team.

As part of the transition to the new structure, Church Treasurer Janice Wenger took the opportunity to retire after 33 years of service in the unpaid position. During that time she not only had paid the bills, but had managed the payroll for the church's burgeoning staff. And during the building project she had taken on significant additional work stemming from the church's decision to function as its own general contractor. Janice retired at the end of 2012, at which point treasurer became a modestly paid position and payroll was outsourced.

Also joining the pastoral staff in 2013 were Director of Youth Ministries Jeffrey Keller and Director of Children's Ministries Janet Myers. About the same time, Carol Ludwig and Liz Rowe were hired as part-time Nursery Directors. Beginning in September 2013, native son Joel Gibbel, who had been licensed by the congregation on September 9, 2012, began a nine-month stint as a student intern, serving 10-14 hours per week as part of his studies through Bethany Theological Seminary.

CHAPTER 8

Where We've Been, Where We're Going

REFLECTIONS FROM 25 YEARS AGO

The 75th anniversary history of the Lititz Church of the Brethren, published in 1990, reflected on the significant changes that had taken place in the church, noting that the church then was hardly the same church that had met in a white frame meetinghouse on Willow Street 75 years before. Strengths that longtime members pointed to in 1989—capable pastors, good music program, nice organ, strong community involvement, modern facilities—weren't even part of the church life 75 years earlier. In fact, nearly all of the things that many members thought made Lititz an attractive congregation in 1989 would have been strongly frowned upon or prohibited in the church's early days. The congregation opposed paying pastors then. Musical instruments and special music weren't part of the congregation's worship. Emphasis was placed on remaining separate from the world, rather than getting involved in the community. By 1989 Lititz Brethren dressed and lived much like the rest of society and separation from the world was no longer valued.

But from where did that new vision come? What created the openness to change that characterized the Lititz church? Several factors may help explain the dramatic changes that took place.

Seeds of change may have been planted in the early years by leaders such as J. W. G. Hershey and Henry R. Gibbel. Though both of these men dedicated their lives to serving and preserving the plain church of their day, they planted the seeds for the outward looking, culture-embracing congregation of later years. Both Hershey and Gibbel were champions of higher education. Beginning with the Hersheys and Gibbels, the congregation sent a steady stream of young people off to college. They returned having been exposed to other cultures, other Christians, other customs. They could no longer accept that their congregation's vision of the church was the only valid vision. Change resulted.

Of course, why the congregation embraced higher education so early is another question. It may have had something to do with the congregation's Lititz location. Though located in conservative Lancaster County, because of its Moravian beginnings Lititz was different from surrounding communities. The town had two exclusive private schools and generally seemed to place more emphasis on "culture" and education. One longtime Lititz member observes, "Some historians have said that the community of Lititz possessed a 'modest egotism' because of cultural and educational opportunities available here through the Moravian Church, the Linden Hall School for Girls, and the Beck School." Then he mused, "Did any of this 'modest egotism' carry over into the Lititz Church of the Brethren?" The affirmative answer was implied in the posing of the question.

A similar outside influence came from new members who joined the church from other denominations or from Brethren congregations outside of Pennsylvania. Florence Gibbel, matriarch of the church, was Lutheran. Mayno Hershey came from a Brethren congregation in Ohio, where many distinctive Brethren features had already declined. She was an advocate for change from the day of her arrival in 1929. Members from other denominations came and participated in the life of the church. They certainly brought different understandings of the church and played a role in shaping the Lititz Church of the Brethren. After the 1958 decision to waive the rebaptism requirement for members from other denominations, this factor probably increased in importance. Today, members observe, while Lititz maintains a strong commitment to denominational identity and involvement in the larger church, a significant portion of the members are local in their focus, with less interest in Brethren identity and less knowledge of and involvement in the work of the denomination.

Pastors have been another impetus for change. It is no coincidence that the emphasis placed on congregational discipline began to wane shortly after the arrival of the first paid pastor in 1935. James Moore brought an urban influence from Chicago. Young Floyd McDowell advocated significant organizational change that had lasting impact after his relatively brief tenure. New pastors brought new ideas. Certainly, the congregation was open to change and could have evolved similarly without the influence of outside pastors; but it seems likely that pastors at least accelerated change.

Ernest Shenk pointed to another probable factor. "I've always felt that Lititz is very willing to let the younger people become active [in leadership]," he said. Jim Gibbel observed that the new plan of organization in 1955 provided more opportunities for young people to take leadership positions in the church. Three of the congregation's pastors also were young: Jacob Dick and Floyd McDowell were 27 when they came, and Clem Rosenberger was in his early thirties. That willingness to entrust younger—and sometimes more progressive—people with responsibility helped shape the congregation.

Whatever the causes, longtime members interviewed a quarter century ago were at peace with what their church had become. Peggy Cassel, who had rebelled against wearing her prayer covering to school in her teenage years, stated, "I don't think they are missing anything today that we had in the past." Now deceased, she was much more at home in the culture-embracing church of her later years than in the church of her youth.

Margaret Krumbine, who since passed away, argued that the church had held on to the basics while changing to meet the needs of a new day. "The basic principles we learned in the old Willow Street and Center Street churches we still have," she said. "Those things are instilled in us and will always be there." She spoke of basics such as living in right relationship with others, honesty, and sincerity.

What About Today?

What about today? What have been the defining trends of the past 25 years and what are their implications for the Lititz Church of the Brethren of today and its future? Several trends are evident:

- Rising professionalism;
- Declining attendance and an aging membership;

- Fewer people guiding the congregation;
- Upgraded facilities;
- Expansion of worship options and new ministries;
- An openness to serving the community.

During the past quarter century, the congregation has seen a marked rise in professionalism, as indicated by a rapidly expanding paid staff and a frequent use of consultants. A century ago, the Lititz Church of the Brethren was an all-volunteer organization. By the mid-1930s the church paid one salaried pastor, and along the way added part-time music staff and a custodian to the payroll. It took the church another 30 years to add a second pastoral staff member. In its 75th anniversary year in 1989, a part-time Pastor for Christian Nurture was added to the team. "The front of our bulletin used to say, 'Jimmy Ross, Pastor, Ralph Moyer, Associate Pastor,'" recalls Joel Gibbel. "And it had the name of our organist. Now our bulletin has like 10 names."

By 2013, the church directory listed more than a dozen full- and part-time paid staff members and 60 percent of the church budget was dedicated to personnel, including five pastoral staff (one of whom was a volunteer), three music staff, and six support staff. Among the support staff were Administrative Assistant Diane Lamborn, Maintenance Manager Don Heisey, Custodian Don Rowe, and Director of Food Services Joanne Nolt. The church also pays Nursery Coordinators, a treasurer, security staff who open and close the building, a bell choir director, and perhaps others. In fairness, many of the positions provide modest pay for very part-time work, but the trend is unmistakable. And the large office suite included in the latest building project gave visible expression to the premium placed on professional staff.

"That's Lititz," observes moderator Jeff Glisson. "Professionalism. Lititz has to do it top-notch and we have to do it with paid staff." The church's penchant for hiring has been accompanied by a decline in volunteerism, a younger member observes. "Many of our older members have volunteered and done a lot of things over the years," he says, "and now they are like, 'We're just tired. Can we pay somebody to do it?'"

Another adds, "The thing is, when you hear about large churches that are really growing, they say you have to hire staff to grow. So we kind of follow and say, 'I guess so.'"

Related to the growth in staff has been a growing penchant for hiring professional consultants to lead the congregation in various forms of planning. Since the early 1990s, when the church concluded Adventure in Mission and Passing on the Promise—two denominational programs aimed at improving stewardship and evangelism, respectively—the Lititz Church has almost constantly been engaged in some kind of goal-setting, strategic planning, or visioning process with the assistance of a professional consultant. Count them: Jim Moss, People Spots; S. Joan Hershey, Florin Church of the Brethren; Stan Dueck, Church of the Brethren Congregational Life Team; Craig Sider, Strategic Pathways Intiative; and Mark DeVries and Nate Stuckey, Youth Ministry Architects. This list doesn't include the more typical use of an architect and decorator during the building project and John H. Miller's services for three capital campaigns. A congregation that includes a wide variety of professionals within its membership and has a large number of qualified professional staff on its payroll still frequently employs additional consultants to provide guidance.

Fewer People Doing More Work

The growth in paid staff has been accompanied by decreased involvement of lay members in providing leadership for the church's ministries. During the past 25 years it grew increasingly difficult to find volunteers to serve on church boards and committees. The Board gradually was downsized, until 2013, when a radical revision to the church's plan of organization was initiated. Among a number of changes, the new plan replaced a larger Church Board with an eight-member Leadership Team. While the purpose of the change was to free people to engage in actual ministries, rather than spending inordinate amounts of time sitting in administrative meetings, the change also concentrated authority in the hands of a small group.

To be sure, the Congregational Meeting remains the final authority and still holds sway over major decisions. And the "permission-giving" philosophy of the new organization intends to free members for ministry without requiring the Leadership Team's stamp of approval. But the trend is clear: A congregation that once embodied democracy with a committee-of-the-whole approach to decision-making gradually ceded authority to smaller and smaller groups within the church. Today, the areas under the purview of the Leadership Team comprise 75 percent of the budget.

Increasing Age and Decreasing Attendance

Another trend members point to has been the aging of the congregation. When today's Leadership Team chair Bri-

In this picture of the 1986/1987 adult choir, Brian Rice (back left) is one of the youngest members. Nearly 30 years later Brian still is among the youngest singers in the group.

an Rice and his wife, Jodie, joined the choir as newlyweds in 1983 they were the youngest voices in the choir. Thirty years later, says Brian, "We're still the youngest ones in the choir." Part of the "aging" of the congregation is a positive trend. Lititz is in close proximity to three retirement communities—Moravian Manor, Luther Acres, and Brethren Village—and has intentionally reached out to retirees by scheduling daytime music programs, providing transportation from Brethren Village for Sunday worship since 2008, and maintaining a strong traditional service that appeals to older generations.

Along with aging, the congregation has experienced a decline in membership and attendance. Since 1990, membership has shrunk from 794 to 705, with 624 of those members considered active. Average worship attendance dropped from 363 to 285, and Sunday school attendance from 283 to 216.

Despite employing a senior pastor with a heart for evangelism and church growth, engaging in intentional visioning and planning to grow the church, offering varieties of worship styles to cater to diverse tastes, initiating a variety of new ministries, and building and maintaining a beautiful facility, numbers have continued to decline. "The biggest gaps," says moderator Jeff Glisson, "are in older children and youth and their parents." While the church brings new people in, he observes, more work can be done at building relationships with new people and fully incorporating them into the life of the church.

In some respects, what Lititz is experiencing isn't all that different from other U.S. mainline churches, who have faced declining membership for decades. The cultural trend, suggests Jeff, is toward less commitment, not more. While a regular attender used to be in church most every week, today some "regular attenders" come one or two Sundays per month. Churches now face more competition than ever on Sundays from sports activities, work commitments, leisure activities, and more. And they also face competition from other churches, which sometimes are more successful at attracting church "consumers" seeking the "worship experience" that appeals to them.

"There are other churches that are vibrant in our community," observes Joel Gibbel. "Some members walk out the back door and we find out later that they're attending elsewhere. . . . And we don't like to talk about that because it makes us insecure that somebody has a 'better' church than us. But that has happened." And while no one will come out and say it, perhaps working through a large building project and wrangling over worship styles and schedules contributed to the loss of some members.

A Future of Promise?

Despite some trends that are cause for concern, the Lititz congregation at age 100 also has some signs pointing to a bright future. In the past 25 years the church has seen a blossoming of outreach and service ministries, unmatched by many other eras of the church. The church has called out ministers, sent volunteers to rebuild homes following disasters, partnered with urban churches, joined hands with brothers and sisters in the Dominican Republic and Haiti, and been a blessing through the giving of time and money to serve in Jesus' name.

Closer to home, the Lititz congregation continues to find ways to be a blessing to the surrounding community, offering its facility for the benefit of others. In an October 2013 *Messenger* article titled "Back to the Future: How one congregation is making its 'meeting house' useful in today's world," Pastor Kettering reflected on the church's changing understanding of its building. In the early years the Lititz Brethren referred to the plain structure on Willow Street as a meetinghouse. Though still somewhat simple, the more Protestant structure on Center Street was called a church or church house. A few referred to the sparkling new building built on the edge of town in 1962 as a "church plant."

In his *Messenger* article, Bob proposed a new term for the current building: Ministry Center. Each church bulletin and newsletter now includes the words "Lititz Church of the Brethren, Ministry Center located at 300 West Orange Street." In the article he made a strong case that the Lititz Brethren are using their facilities for precisely this purpose. Bob wrote:

> I have come to realize that the structure that our congregation owns is a tremendous tool for

ministry and mission in our community. I am grateful for the large and versatile structure where I serve. . . . I am even more grateful for a congregation who has for years seen this building as a place for mission and ministry, not just for our congregation for [sic] but for a whole host of other groups.

And then he listed the dizzying number of activities that take place at the Ministry Center: worship services, love feasts, Holy Week services, Bible studies, prayer groups, Wednesday Nights ALIVE, Summer Kidz ALIVE, New Year's Day dinners, musical events, quilting for disaster relief, day care, Faith and Friendship Club, Toddler Gym, Scouts, Meals on Wheels, age group activities, TNT youth ministry, square dancing, and an array of other recreational activities.

Bob continued:

> While it is true we have a large, versatile, and beautiful building, the Lititz congregation has a very generous attitude about sharing our facility with the community for recreation, fellowship, outreach, mission, and ministry. To our way of thinking, our building should be used as much as possible every day and evening of the week.

The jury is still out on whether anyone other than Bob will take to calling the church building a Ministry Center. But whether the new nomenclature catches on may not matter. Whatever they call it, the Lititz church obviously already views its building as a center for ministry. Although they have some concerns for the future as they begin their second century, the Lititz Brethren have good reason to believe many good years lie ahead. Not only does the Lititz Church of the Brethren have much to celebrate from its first century of ministry, but its magnificent facilities, generous spirit, and outward focus all bode well for a future of promise.

Appendix A
Ministers and Moderators

Free Ministers, 1914-1932

John W. Myer, Sr.
J. W. G. Hershey
Henry R. Gibbel

Harvey M. Eberly
John W. Hevener
John I. Byler, Sr.

Pastors, 1932-Present

1932-1935	A. C. Baugher (part-time)
1935-1945	James M. Moore
1945-1952	Jacob T. Dick
1947	Kenneth Frantz, Summer Pastor
1952	Lowell Zuck, Interim Pastor
1952-1955	Earl M. Bowman
1955-1959	E. Floyd McDowell
1959-1966	Olden D. Mitchell
1964-1973	D. Howard Keiper, Minister of Visitation
1966-1982	W. Clemens Rosenberger
1969-1978	Arlin G. Claassen, Associate Pastor
1978-1979	Robert L. Life, Interim Associate Pastor
1980-1998	Ralph Z. Moyer, Pastor for Special Ministries
1982-1983	Howard W. Bernhard, Minister of Visitation
1983-1998	Jimmy R. Ross
1987	Rebecca Baile Crouse, Summer Pastoral Intern
1989-1994	Henry L. Renn, Pastor for Christian Nurture
1994-2000	Tracy Wenger Sadd, Pastor for Christian Nurture

1998	Robert D. Kettering, (Interim Associate Pastor, Interim Pastor)
1999-	Robert D. Kettering
1998-1999	Dana E. Statler, Interim Associate Pastor
1999-	Stephen R. Hess, Associate Pastor
1999-2002	Janice Havemann, Director of Youth Ministries
2000-2008	Pamela A. Reist, Director of Christian Nurture, Pastor of Christian Nurture, Associate Pastor
2003-2005	James J. Koser, Director of Youth Ministries
2007-	Ralph Z. Moyer, Volunteer Pastor of Visitation
2008-2012	Deborah E. Evans, Director of Christian Nurture
2013-	Jeffrey Keller, Director of Youth Ministries
2013-	Janet C. Myers, Director of Children's Ministries
2013-2014	Joel C. Gibbel, Pastoral Intern

Elders-In-Charge and Moderators

1914-1919	Isaac W. Taylor	1972-1978	Elwood H. Gibble
1919-1929	J. W. G. Hershey	1979-1981	Harry H. Badorf
1929-1932	Nathan Martin	1982-1984	Henry G. Bucher
1932-1933	John I. Byler	1985-1987	Larry D. Sauder
1933-1936	A. C. Baugher	1988-1993	Jefferson C. Crosby
1936-1945	James M. Moore	1994-1999	James C. Gibbel
1945-1961	Norman K. Musser	2000-2002	Henry H. Gibbel
1961-1966	Henry G. Bucher	2003-2008	James C. Gibbel
1966-1972	John G. Hershey	2009-	Jeffrey H. Glisson

The term "moderator" replaced "elder-in-charge" or "presiding elder" when a new plan of organization was adopted in 1955. Norman Musser was the last elder-in-charge and the first moderator.

APPENDIX A: MINISTERS AND MODERATORS   219

A. C. Baugher    James M. Moore    Jacob T. Dick

Earl M. Bowman    E. Floyd McDowell    Olden D. Mitchell

D. Howard Keiper    W. Clemens Rosenberger    Arlin C. Claassen

Ralph Z. Moyer  *Jimmy R. Ross*  *Henry L. Renn*

Tracy Wenger Sadd  *Robert D. Kettering*  *Stephen R. Hess*

Pamela A. Reist  *Janet C. Myers*  *Jeffrey Keller*

APPENDIX B

Key Events

1887	The West Conestoga congregation (now Middle Creek) erects a meetinghouse in Lititz.
April 1903	West Conestoga approves the organization of a Sunday school at the Lititz meetinghouse.
January 1914	Lititz Brethren organized as a separate congregation.
December 1914	Congregation baptizes its first new members.
March 1922	First Vacation Bible School approved.
1926	New church erected on Center Street.
July 1932	Congregation votes to employ a part-time pastor.
1934	First congregational directory printed.
May 1935	Congregation calls first full-time pastor, approves first budget.
October 1935	Voted to participate in community Thanksgiving service.
September 1938	Approved the use of individual communion cups.
March 1939	Permission granted to have musical instrument in church.
August 1939	Voted to build first church parsonage.
February 1940	Voted to install first baptismal pool in the Center Street church.
March 1940	Annual deacon visit is discontinued.
April 1951	Organ in sanctuary is dedicated.
September 1951	Congregation approves "open communion."
August 1955	Adopted new plan of organization: Board of Administration replaces Official Board.
May 1957	Approved employment of part-time church secretary.

November 1957	Congregation adopts first unified budget.
April 1958	Elected first term deacons.
October 1958	Voted to accept non-Brethren as new members without rebaptizing them.
September 1961	Approved first bread and cup communion service.
June 1962	New church on Orange Street dedicated.
1964	Church begins sponsorship of Boy Scout Troop #154.
July 1965	Pavilion dedicated.
November 1967	Youth Club begins.
May 1968	Congregation agrees to hire first full-time associate pastor.
March 1969	New parsonage completed.
September 1969	New fellowship hall and chapel dedicated.
October 1970	Historic District Conference held at Lititz—Atlantic Northeast District formed from Eastern and North Atlantic Districts.
September 1972	Congregation receives pew Bibles.
1973	Congregation begins hosting Meals on Wheels program
June 1983	First Lititz Run for Peace.
1988	Bell choir organized.
1989	Lititz congregation celebrates 75th anniversary.
September 1991	Partnership with Lititz Rec Center to operate day care in church begins.
July 1992	*Hymnal: A Worship Book* (blue hymnal) used in worship for first time.
May 1994	Adoption of 10-year plan growing out of People Spots process.
April 1995	Church begins second worship service, meeting at 8:00 a.m.
May 1999	Vote to form Facility Improvement Committee.
January 2000	First annual New Year's Day pork and sauerkraut dinner to support recently created Youth Foundation Fund.
October 2000	Beginning of Wednesday Nights ALIVE program.
March 2002	First "Music at Mid-Month" concert.
October 2002	Toddler Gym program begins.
November 2002	First child protection policy approved.

APPENDIX B: KEY EVENTS

April 2003	Groundbreaking for $3.7 million building project.
April 2003	First church website launched.
October 2003	Monthly Men's Fellowship Breakfast begins.
July 2004	Recently installed Peace Pole is dedicated.
September 2004	Contemporary worship service implemented.
April 2005	Building Dedication/90th anniversary celebration.
October 2006	Memorial Garden dedicated.
June 2010	Chapel service discontinued, leaving one traditional and one contemporary service.
February 2012	TNT Youth Center begins meeting at Lititz.
June 2012	Board approves new child protection policy.
October 2012	Congregation retires building debt and is totally debt free.
December 2012	Refurbished and expanded organ dedicated.
January 2013	New plan of organization begins. Leadership Team replaces Board.
July 2013	Congregation hosts first Karen worship service in chapel.
2014	Events throughout the year to celebrate 100th anniversary.

APPENDIX C
Membership and Average Attendance

Year	Total Members	Active Members	Worship Attendance	Sunday School Attendance
1914	119			
1919	165			
1924	247			
1929	226			
1934	267			
1939	368			
1944*	419		247	
1949	468		274	
1954	496		274	
1959	568		318	354
1964	612		380	376
1969	675		355	305
1974	716		274	370
1979	767		356	255
1984	784		372	279
1989	784		368	274
1994	772	601	385	299
1999	768	620	374	279
2004	806	693	377	273
2009	712	640	325	256
2013	706	624	284	216

* *Data not available for 1944. Membership figure is from 1945, Worship Attendance from 1947.*

Sources: Congregational directories and Council minutes.

APPENDIX D

100th Anniversary Celebration Events

January 1 **Pork and Sauerkraut Dinner**
Anniversary Kickoff and Support for Youth Foundation Fund
11:00 am – 3:00 pm

January 12 **Celebration with the Middle Creek Congregation**
Hymn Sing, Worship, and Fellowship Time
3:00 pm

February 2 **Heritage Sunday Reflecting a 1914 Worship Service**
Ralph Moyer, Pastor for Special Ministries, 1980-1998, Preaching
9:00 am

March 2 **Spiritual Renewal Services**
Donald Kraybill, Senior Fellow, Elizabethtown College Young Center
9:00 am and 6:30 pm Worship
(Evening service snowed out)

April 6	**Sunday Morning Worship** Arlin Claassen, Associate Pastor, 1969-1978, Preaching 9:00 am and 9:15 am
April 17	**Love Feast and Communion Service** Led by Jeff Bach, Director, Elizabethtown College Young Center 6:00 pm
May 3	**Celebration Weekend** A Gathering for Fellowship, Remembering, and Sharing a Meal Together 5:00 pm
May 4	**Celebration Weekend** A Gathering for Worship with Earl Ziegler Preaching 9:00 am
June 8	**Heritage Tour of Former Meetinghouses and Baptismal Site** 2:00 pm
August 3	**Sunday Morning Worship** Jimmy Ross, Pastor, 1983-1998, Preaching 9:00 am and 9:15 am
September 14	**Children and Youth Worship Service** 9:00 am

October 19   **A Future of Promise**
Jeffrey Carter, President, Bethany Theological Seminary, Preaching
A Gathering for Worship as We Look to the Future in Continuing in the Footsteps of Jesus
9:00 am

November 2   **Remembrance Sunday**
Pamela Reist, Associate Pastor, 2000-2008, Preaching
9:00 am

November 16   **Mission Sunday**
A Celebration of Lititz's Mission and Service Ministry
9:00 am

Sources Consulted

A Pictorial History of Lititz. Lititz: Express Printing Company, 1905.

Bowman, Earl McKinley. *An Unknown Parson.* Verona, Va.: Earl M. Bowman, 1976.

Eastern District of Pennsylvania Historical Committee. *History of the Church of the Brethren of the Eastern District of Pennsylvania.* Lancaster, Pa.: Historical Committee, 1915.

Fitzkee, Donald R. *Moving Toward the Mainstream: 20th Century Change Among the Brethren of Eastern Pennsylvania.* Intercourse, Pa.: Good Books, 1995.

Fitzkee, Donald R. *The Transformation of the Lititz Church of the Brethren, 1914-1989.* Lititz: Lititz Church of the Brethren, 1990.

Saylor, Guy R., Ed. *History of the Church of the Brethren, Eastern Pennsylvania, 1915-1965.* Lancaster: Eastern District of Pennsylvania, 1965.

Primary Sources

The congregation published booklets that contained a brief history of the church for its 50th anniversary in 1964 and its 60th anniversary in 1974.

Building Dedication Program, 1926.

Congregational Directories.

Council Meeting minutes and Board Meeting minutes.

The Lititz Messenger (church newsletters), 1936-1948.

The Lititz Observer (church newsletters), 1956-2014.

Interviews Conducted in 1989
by Donald Fitzkee

Harry Badorf
Laura (Hershey) Barwick
Ada Bingeman
Franklin & Peggy Cassel
James Gibbel
Elwood Gibble
Mayno Hershey

Floyd McDowell
Beatrice Mohler
W. Clemens Rosenberger
Ernest & Marian Shenk
Janet (Garman) Smith
Landis Stehman
Levi and Mary Weaver

Pastors Interviewed on Video in 2013
by Becky Hershey Becker

Steve Hess
Robert Kettering
Ralph Moyer
Pamela Reist

Henry Renn
Jimmy Ross *(interviewed jointly with Donald Fitzkee)*
Tracy Wenger Sadd

Group Interviews Conducted
by Donald Fitzkee in 2013

History: Becky Hershey Becker, James Gibbel, Verna Moseman
Recent Changes: Joel Gibbel, Jeff Glisson, Cindy Martin, Brian Rice
Building Committee Members: Fritz Blough, Marty Hershey, Kenneth Hess